YOUR recipe could appear in our next cookbook!

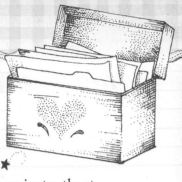

Share your tried & true family favorites with us instantly at

www.gooseberrypatch.com

If you'd rather jot 'em down by hand, just mail this form to...

Gooseberry Patch • Cookbooks – Call for Recipes
2500 Farmers Dr., #110 • Columbus, OH 43235

If your recipe is selected for a book, you'll receive a FREE copy!

Please share only your original recipes or those that you have made your own over the years.

Recipe Name:

Number of Servings:

Any fond memories about this recipe? Special touches you like to add
or handy shortcuts?

Ingredients (include specific measurements):

D0713593

Instructions (continue on back if needed):

Special Code: **cookbookspage**

Extra space for recipe if needed:

Tell us about yourself...

Your complete contact information is needed so that we can send you your FREE cookbook, if your recipe is published. Phone numbers and email addresses are kept private and will only be used if we have questions about your recipe.

Name:

Address:

City: State: Zip:

Email:

Daytime Phone:

Thank you! Vickie & Jo Ann

HOMETOWN
Harvest

Gooseberry Patch
2500 Farmers Dr., #110
Columbus, OH 43235

www.gooseberrypatch.com

1·800·854·6673

Copyright 2013, Gooseberry Patch 978-1-62093-027-4
Fourth Printing, June, 2013

Check out our cooking videos on YouTube!

 Scan this code with your smartphone or tablet...it takes you
right to our YouTube playlist of cooking videos for **Hometown
Harvest**. While there, you can also view our entire collection
of **Gooseberry Patch** cooking videos!

 If you spot this icon next to a recipe name, it means we
created a video for it. You'll find it at **www.youtube.com/
gooseberrypatchcom**.

Contents

Dedication

To everyone who still jumps
in piles of leaves, loves sticky
caramel apples and relaxes
with a cup of hot cider.

Appreciation

A warm and heartfelt thanks
to those who shared their best
fall recipes and memories with
us...we owe this book to you.

HOMETOWN
Pancake Breakfast

Perfectly Pumpkin Pancakes

Amy Bradsher
Roxboro, NC

My son Luke loves pumpkin! In the fall, we make our own fresh pumpkin purée together. Although he's only four, he loves scooping out the insides and running them through the food mill. These pancakes keep him full of energy!

3 c. whole-wheat flour	1/8 t. ground ginger
2 T. brown sugar, packed	15-oz. can pumpkin
2 t. baking soda	2 c. buttermilk
3/4 t. kosher salt	1/2 c. milk
1 t. cinnamon	3 eggs, beaten

In a large bowl, stir together flour, brown sugar, baking soda, salt and spices. Add remaining ingredients and stir until just moistened. Let stand for several minutes to allow batter to rise. Pour batter by 1/4 cupfuls onto a hot buttered griddle over medium heat. When edges are golden, turn and cook other side. Pancakes will be very thick and may need to be turned a third time to make sure the centers are done. Makes 8 to 10 pancakes.

The air is brisk and the leaves are turning...it's autumn! Invite family & friends to a cozy brunch, then take everyone to a nearby park for a leaf hike. It's a wonderful time for food and fun.

German Apple Pancake

Gail Blain Prather
Hastings, NE

This German breakfast treat is sometimes called a Puff Pancake or Dutch Baby...whatever you call it, it's a fall staple at our house! It's yummy served with a side of crisp thick-sliced bacon.

3 to 4 T. butter
6 Granny Smith apples, cored
    and thinly sliced
1/3 c. sugar
nutmeg to taste

6 eggs, beaten
1 c. milk
1/2 t. vanilla extract
1 c. all-purpose flour
Garnish: warm maple syrup

In an 8" cast-iron skillet over medium heat, melt butter and sauté apple slices. Sprinkle with sugar and nutmeg; cook until sugar is dissolved and apples begin to soften. In a bowl, whisk together eggs, milk, vanilla and flour; pour mixture over apples. Transfer skillet to oven. Bake, uncovered, at 375 degrees for 20 to 30 minutes, until puffed and set in the center. Cut into wedges; serve warm with syrup. Serves 6.

A hearty breakfast for the chilliest morning! Cook up
diced potatoes in a cast-iron skillet, then make six wells with the
back of a spoon. Break an egg into each well, cover and cook
for a few minutes more, until eggs are set. Serve piping hot,
right from the skillet.

Lawerence's Alphabet Pancakes

Karolyn Duponcheel
Ainsworth, NE

When our oldest son was small, he loved to help me cook. He thought of this recipe when pancake batter was in the skillet before the rest of the batter was poured. We had many chuckles when he discovered the initials had to be poured backwards!

6 eggs, beaten
3 c. milk
2 c. all-purpose flour

2 t. baking powder
3/4 t. salt
1 t. butter, melted

Combine eggs and milk in a bowl; whisk well. Add flour, baking powder and salt; beat until smooth. Stir in butter. With a large spoon, quickly pour or drizzle a small amount of batter onto a greased, heated griddle to form initials or a name (remember to work backwards). Cook until lightly golden. Pour 1/2 cup batter over initials. Cook until golden; turn and cook on other side. Makes 12 to 15 pancakes.

Serve pancakes with cheery pumpkin faces! Cut an apple into thin slices, then cut triangles for the eyes and nose. Give Jack a happy smile with an apple slice for his mouth. Don't forget to dip the apple slices in lemon juice to keep them from browning.

Maudeen's Blackberry Gravy

LuLu Combs
Aberdeen, MD

My mother-in-law was an awesome country cook. She taught me how to do many things, but the best lesson was how to make country-style biscuits & gravy. Every once in a while, she'd open up a jar of home-canned blackberries and make this wonderful sauce to enjoy with her homemade biscuits. I hope you enjoy it as much as my family does!

1/2 c. sugar	1 c. water
1/4 c. all-purpose flour	2 T. butter
12-oz. pkg. frozen blackberries	8 to 12 biscuits, split

Combine sugar and flour in a bowl; mix well and set aside. In a saucepan over medium-high heat, bring blackberries and water to a boil. Add sugar mixture; stir well. Cook and stir to desired consistency, adding a little more water if gravy is too thick. Remove from heat; stir in butter. Serve over warm biscuits. Makes 8 to 12 servings.

I cannot endure to waste anything
as precious as autumn sunshine
by staying in the house.

–Nathaniel Hawthorne

Buttermilk Pecan Waffles

*Nancy Girard
Chesapeake, VA*

A wonderful way to start an autumn morning...such a treat!

1 c. all-purpose flour
3/4 t. baking powder
1/4 t. baking soda
1-1/2 T. sugar
1/8 t. salt

2 eggs, separated
1 c. buttermilk
3 T. butter, melted and slightly
    cooled
1/3 c. chopped pecans, toasted

In a bowl, stir together flour, baking powder, baking soda, sugar and salt; set aside. In a separate bowl, beat egg whites with an electric mixer on high speed until soft peaks form. In a separate large bowl, beat egg yolks, buttermilk and butter. Add flour mixture to egg yolk mixture; stir just until smooth. Fold in egg whites and pecans just until blended. Pour batter by 1/2 cupfuls onto a heated waffle iron; bake according to manufacturer's instructions. Makes 2 waffles.

Fall is sweater weather, so keep a cozy sweater on a hook
near the back door and enjoy an early-morning walk
uptown after breakfast.

Autumn Apple Waffles

Robin Windecker
Ponchatoula, LA

My children just love these waffles for a scrumptious
get-warm breakfast on a cold day.

2 c. milk
2 eggs, beaten
1/4 c. butter, melted and slightly
   cooled
2 c. pancake mix
1 t. cinnamon

1 c. Golden Delicious apples,
   peeled, cored and finely
   chopped
Garnish: maple syrup or
   powdered sugar

Combine milk, eggs, butter, pancake mix and cinnamon in a large bowl. Beat until batter is smooth. Fold in apples. Pour batter by 1/4 cupfuls onto a heated waffle iron; bake according to manufacturer's instructions. Serve topped with maple syrup or dusted with powdered sugar. Makes about 4 waffles.

Boiled cider is a terrific topping for pancakes or oatmeal... desserts too. It's simple to make. Pour 2 quarts apple cider into a heavy saucepan. Bring to a boil, then reduce heat and simmer gently for 1-3/4 hours, until cider has boiled down to 1-1/2 cups. Cool; refrigerate in a wide-mouth jar.

Skillet Apples & Sausages

Sue Klapper
Muskego, WI

The apples and brown sugar give these sausages such a delicious sweetness...a great side dish for a brunch!

1 lb. pork breakfast sausage
   links
6 Cortland or Golden Delicious
   apples, cored and cut into
   8 wedges

3 T. brown sugar, packed
1 T. lemon juice
1/4 t. salt
1/8 t. pepper

In a large skillet, cook sausages over medium heat for about 10 minutes, until no longer pink inside. Drain; cut sausages in half and return to skillet. Add apple wedges. Sprinkle with remaining ingredients. Cover and cook over medium-low heat for 10 to 15 minutes, until apples are just tender, gently stirring once or twice. Serves 6.

Colorful oilcloth is so pretty as a table covering and has the added bonus of being quick & easy to clean. Ideal when breakfast calls for sticky syrup or honey!

Harvest Hot White Chocolate

Crystal Shook
Catawba, NC

My daughter Cora asks for this hot chocolate all year long.
Serve in clear glass coffee mugs...very pretty!

15-oz. can pumpkin
14-oz. can sweetened condensed
   milk
4 c. whole milk
1 t. vanilla extract

1 t. pumpkin pie spice
1-1/4 c. white chocolate chips
Garnish: whipped cream,
   pumpkin pie spice,
   cinnamon sticks

In a large saucepan, combine pumpkin, milks, vanilla and spice;
whisk well. Bring to a simmer over medium heat, stirring frequently.
Add chocolate chips; stir until melted. Pour into mugs; garnish with
whipped cream, a sprinkle of spice and a cinnamon stick for stirring.
Makes 6 to 8 servings.

Autumn Morning Smoothie

Julie Dossantos
Fort Pierce, FL

Our family loves to make breakfast smoothies. After baking pie
pumpkins, I decided to try making smoothies for Thanksgiving
morning. They were a hit! Now we enjoy them all autumn.

1/2 c. fresh pumpkin purée or
   canned pumpkin
3/4 c. papaya, peeled, seeded
   and cubed
2 bananas, sliced

1/2 c. low-fat vanilla yogurt
1/4 c. orange juice
4 ice cubes
1-1/2 t. cinnamon
Garnish: additional cinnamon

Add all ingredients except garnish to a blender. Process until smooth;
pour into 2 tall glasses. Top each with a sprinkle of cinnamon. Serves 2.

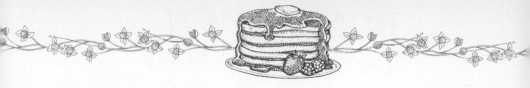

Cranberry-Orange Strata

Anna McMaster
Portland, OR

My friend Carol brought me a gift jar of orange marmalade from England. It was too special to just spread on toast! I found this recipe and it was perfect...everyone at my pre-game brunch loved it.

12 slices bread, divided
1-1/2 c. cream cheese, softened
1-1/2 t. orange zest
9 eggs
3 c. half-and-half
2 T. sugar

2 t. vanilla extract
1 c. sweetened dried cranberries, divided
1/2 c. chopped walnuts
1 c. orange marmalade
1/4 c. orange juice

Arrange 6 slices bread in a lightly greased 13"x9" baking pan; set aside. In a large bowl, blend cream cheese and orange zest with an electric mixer on low speed. Beat in eggs, one at a time. Add half-and-half, sugar and vanilla; beat on medium speed until smooth. Spoon one cup cream cheese mixture over bread in pan; sprinkle with 1/2 cup cranberries. Arrange remaining bread slices on top; spoon remaining cream cheese mixture over top. Cover and let stand for 30 minutes. Uncover; sprinkle with walnuts and remaining cranberries, lightly pressing down. Bake, uncovered, at 325 degrees for 35 to 40 minutes, until puffy and set. Let stand for 10 minutes. In a small saucepan over low heat, cook and stir marmalade and orange juice. Cut strata into squares; drizzle with warm marmalade mixture. Serves 8 to 10.

Just for fun, serve bottles of juice and milk tucked into a pumpkin-turned-ice bucket! Cut the top third off of a large pumpkin and clean out the inside. Line the pumpkin with a plastic bowl, then fill with ice and beverage containers.

Banana-Stuffed French Toast

*Charlotte Smith
Tyrone, PA*

*Don't settle for ordinary French toast. This recipe is
wonderful...absolutely delicious!*

6 eggs
1/4 c. milk
4 very ripe bananas
1/4 c. chopped walnuts

1/8 t. nutmeg
8 slices French bread, divided
Garnish: powdered sugar,
   jam or maple syrup

In a large shallow bowl, beat eggs and milk; set aside. Place bananas in
a small bowl and mash with a fork; stir in walnuts and nutmeg. Spread
banana mixture over 4 bread slices; top with remaining bread and press
down to seal. Dip each sandwich into egg mixture to coat. On a large
greased griddle over medium heat, cook sandwiches on both sides until
golden. Slice sandwiches on the diagonal. Dust with powdered sugar,
or serve with jam or maple syrup. Makes 4 servings.

Cabin-shaped maple syrup tins make whimsical candleholders
for the breakfast table. Tuck tapers into the opening
and arrange in a group.

15

Autumn Egg Bake

Julie Dossantos
Fort Pierce, FL

We love eating breakfast for dinner. This is a great dish to prepare ahead of time and pop in the oven any time of day! Serve with warm pumpkin muffins for a yummy autumn meal.

6 eggs
4 egg whites
1-1/2 t. nutmeg
6 slices turkey bacon, crisply
   cooked and crumbled

1 c. fresh baby spinach
1/2 c. shredded Parmesan cheese
1/4 c. onion, diced
salt and pepper to taste

In a bowl, beat together eggs, egg whites and nutmeg. Pour into an 11"x9" baking pan sprayed with non-stick vegetable spray. Add remaining ingredients; stir gently. Bake, uncovered, at 350 degrees for 20 to 25 minutes, until eggs are cooked through. Serves 4 to 6.

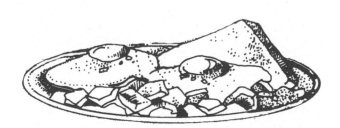

Many farmers' markets are open through the fall season, so don't miss out on all the goodies for a harvest breakfast. You'll find fresh eggs, syrup, potatoes for hashbrowns or potato cakes and loads of other veggies for a tasty omelet or quiche.

Crustless Southwestern Quiche

Cinde Shields
Issaquah, WA

Quiche is always a winner at my house...you can add just about anything you like with delicious results! This warm, satisfying quiche makes the most of your harvest. If you have garden-fresh corn and vine-ripened tomatoes on hand, by all means use them.

4 eggs, beaten
1 c. milk
1/4 c. fresh cilantro, chopped
1/2 t. chili powder
1/4 t. salt
1/4 t. pepper

1 c. frozen corn, thawed
1 tomato, chopped
1-1/4 c. shredded sharp Cheddar cheese
1/4 c. crumbled Cotija cheese or shredded Parmesan cheese

Spray a 9" glass pie plate with non-stick cooking spray. In a bowl, combine eggs, milk and seasonings; stir until blended. Stir in corn, tomato and cheeses; pour into pie plate. Bake at 350 degrees for 40 to 50 minutes, until a knife tip inserted in the center comes out clean. Let stand 10 minutes; cut into wedges. Serves 6.

Start a tailgating Saturday right...invite friends to join you for breakfast! Keep it simple with a breakfast casserole, baskets of muffins and a fresh fruit salad on the menu. It's all about food and friends!

Quinoa Breakfast Bake

Lori Haines
Johnson City, TN

It's terrific to have this casserole tucked in the freezer to serve at a moment's notice! The original recipe came from a B & B. I've changed some of the ingredients to fit my family's taste.

2 lbs. ground pork breakfast
   sausage, browned and
   drained
16-oz. pkg. shredded Colby Jack
   cheese

3 c. cooked quinoa
1 c. milk
4 eggs, beaten
1 T. dried oregano
1 t. garlic, minced

Mix all ingredients in a bowl. Spoon into an 11"x9" baking pan sprayed with non-stick vegetable spray. Bake, uncovered, at 350 degrees for one hour. Let cool slightly; cut into squares and serve warm. To freeze, wrap squares in plastic wrap; store in a plastic freezer bag in the freezer. To reheat, microwave individual squares for 2 minutes. Makes 18 to 24 servings.

Egg Muffins

Christine Gordon
British Columbia, Canada

These breakfast bites are perfect for potlucks...even for road trips! Feel free to use any vegetable you like (even salsa!) and cooked sausage or ham instead of bacon. Yum!

3 eggs, beaten
1/4 c. milk
1/3 c. shredded Cheddar cheese

1/3 c. corn or green pepper, diced
1/4 c. bacon, crisply cooked and
   crumbled

In a bowl, whisk together eggs and milk; mix in remaining ingredients. Spray 6 regular muffin cups or 18 mini muffin cups with non-stick vegetable spray. Spoon egg mixture into muffin cups. Bake at 350 degrees for about 20 minutes, until set. Cool in pan 5 minutes before removing. Makes 6 muffins or 18 mini muffins.

Spinach & Egg Casserole

Jill Weisinger
Murrieta, CA

My mom used to make this dish for special occasions. I just loved it and would try to get her to serve it more often. It can be prepared the night before and just popped into the oven the next morning.

2 T. butter
9 eggs, beaten
1/2 c. milk
1/2 c. sour cream

1 c. shredded Cheddar cheese
1-1/2 c. fresh baby spinach
salt and pepper to taste

Place butter in a 9"x9" baking pan; melt in a 350-degree oven. Mix remaining ingredients in a bowl; pour into pan. Bake, uncovered, at 350 degrees for 30 minutes, or until eggs are set. Serves 6.

Good-news placemats for the breakfast table will get everyone off to a sunny start! On a backing of construction paper, arrange clippings of cheerful stories, sweet or funny pictures, favorite comic strips...whatever amuses you. Cover with a layer of self-adhesive clear plastic and enjoy everyday.

Hashbrown Skillet Omelet

Paula Zsiray
Logan, UT

While visiting in Jackson, Wyoming about 30 years ago, we had a breakfast similar to this at a local restaurant. We liked it so much that I came up with this recipe when we got home. We've been enjoying it ever since!

2 T. oil
3 c. frozen shredded hashbrowns
1/2 lb. bacon, crisply cooked and crumbled
1-1/2 c. shredded Cheddar or Cheddar Jack cheese, divided

6 eggs, beaten
1/4 c. water
1 T. fresh parsley, chopped
1/2 t. paprika
Garnish: hot pepper sauce, catsup

Heat oil in a cast-iron skillet over medium heat. Add frozen hashbrowns; cook for about 10 minutes without turning, until golden. Turn carefully; cook other side until golden. Remove skillet from heat. Sprinkle hashbrowns with bacon and one cup shredded cheese. Beat eggs and water; pour over cheese. Sprinkle with parsley and paprika. Transfer skillet to oven. Bake, uncovered, at 350 degrees for about 20 to 25 minutes, until eggs are set in the center. Remove from oven; sprinkle with remaining cheese and let stand for 5 minutes. Cut into wedges; garnish as desired. Serves 6.

Pack up breakfast and take your family to a nearby park for a sunrise picnic filled with rosy skies and singing birds... you'll have the park all to yourselves!

HOMETOWN
Pancake Breakfast

Bacon, Potato & Leek Frittata

Cindy Jamieson
Ontario, Canada

Frittatas are a family favorite for special-occasion breakfasts.
This one is filled with flavors we're all crazy about!

6 slices bacon, finely chopped
1 to 2 potatoes, peeled and diced
1 leek, halved and sliced
6 eggs, beaten

1/4 c. half-and-half
1/4 t. salt
1/4 t. pepper
1/4 c. shredded Parmesan cheese

In a cast-iron skillet, cook bacon over medium heat until partially cooked but not crisp. Add potatoes and leek to skillet; cook until potatoes are tender and bacon is crisp. Lower heat to medium-low. In a bowl, whisk eggs with half-and-half, salt and pepper. Slowly pour egg mixture into skillet; stir to mix and sprinkle with Parmesan. Continue cooking over medium-high heat until bottom begins to set, 5 to 10 minutes. Transfer skillet to top rack of oven. Bake, uncovered, at 350 degrees for 10 to 15 minutes, until eggs are set and cheese is golden. Cool slightly; cut into wedges. Makes 6 servings.

For a centerpiece in a jiffy, visit your backyard, clip branches
with colorful leaves or sprays of berries and tuck them into vases.
Red or yellow leaves look especially pretty in vintage
milk glass containers.

Bacon & Egg Burrito

Becky Hughes
Delaware, OH

*Perfect for a grab & go breakfast on a busy back-to-school day!
To speed up the cubed potato, microwave it for several minutes
before adding to the skillet.*

2 T. oil
1 potato, peeled and cut into
    1/2-inch cubes
2 T. onion, diced
2 slices bacon, crisply cooked
    and crumbled
2 eggs, beaten

salt and pepper to taste
10-inch flour tortilla, warmed
paprika to taste
1 c. shredded Cheddar cheese
Garnish: sour cream, salsa,
    chopped fresh chives

Heat oil in a skillet over medium-high heat. Add potato and onion; cook
for 2 to 3 minutes, until potato is tender. Add bacon, eggs, salt and
pepper. Cook until eggs are set, stirring occasionally. Place warmed
tortilla on a plate; spoon egg mixture onto tortilla. Sprinkle with paprika;
top with cheese and roll up. Garnish as desired. Makes one serving.

Jams, jellies and preserves keep well, so stock up on homemade
local specialties whenever you travel. They'll be scrumptious
on breakfast muffins and biscuits. Later, you can use them
to bake up yummy jam bars and thumbprint cookies.

Erin's Eggchiladas

Erin Vogler
Spencerport, NY

I was trying to find a way to combine my favorite cuisine (Mexican) with my favorite mealtime (breakfast). This recipe came to me in a moment I can only call a revelation!

1 lb. ground pork breakfast
    sausage
8 eggs, beaten
1 T. butter
16-oz. pkg. shredded sharp
    Cheddar cheese, divided

2 10-oz. cans enchilada sauce,
    divided
16-oz. jar favorite salsa, divided
12 8-inch corn tortillas, warmed

Brown sausage in a skillet over medium heat; drain. In a separate skillet over medium-low heat, lightly scramble eggs in butter. In a bowl, combine sausage, eggs and 1/4 cup cheese; set aside. Spoon a thin layer of enchilada sauce over the bottom of a lightly greased 13"x9" baking pan. Fill each warmed tortilla with a scoop of egg mixture, a heaping tablespoon of salsa and a tablespoon of cheese. Roll up tortillas and place in baking pan, seam-side down. Spoon remaining salsa and enchilada sauce over top. Sprinkle with remaining cheese. Bake, uncovered, at 375 degrees for 15 to 20 minutes, until heated through and cheese is melted. Serves 6.

Make a corncob printed tablecloth...fun for kids to do! Cut or break an ear of dried corn in half to reveal a flower shape. Pour fabric paint in a paper plate and stamp on a plain tablecloth. Leaves may be added with a shape cut from a kitchen sponge.

Cranberry-Eggnog Monkey Bread

Brittany Smith
San Antonio, TX

*I love to give classics a facelift...this is my yummy spin
on an old-fashioned goodie!*

3 7-1/2 oz. tubes refrigerated
   biscuits
1 c. sugar
2 t. cinnamon
2 c. sweetened dried cranberries

1/2 c. butter
1 c. brown sugar, packed
1 c. powdered sugar
3 T. eggnog
1/4 t. vanilla extract

Separate biscuits; cut each into quarters. Combine sugar and cinnamon
in a bowl; coat biscuit pieces in mixture. Arrange 1/3 of the biscuit
pieces in the bottom of a generously greased Bundt® pan. Sprinkle with
1/3 of the dried cranberries. Repeat with 2 more layers, ending with
berries on top. In a small saucepan over low heat, melt butter with
brown sugar. Bring to a boil; cook and stir for one minute. Drizzle over
layered biscuits. Bake at 350 degrees for 35 minutes. Cool in pan on a
wire rack for 10 minutes; invert onto a serving plate. Let cool slightly.
In a small bowl, blend together remaining ingredients; drizzle over top.
Slice and serve.

Fill the house with a delicious aroma. Save orange peels
from breakfast, cut into strips and let dry. Drop a few strips
of peel into a small saucepan of water along with some
whole cloves and cinnamon sticks. Bring to a low simmer...
the spicy scent will be irresistible.

Signe's Cinnamon Chip Scones

Corinne Gross
Tigard, OR

This recipe was given to me by my dear friend Signe.
She is no longer with us, but when I make these delicious scones
I feel like she is with me in the kitchen.

2 c. all-purpose flour
3 T. sugar
1-1/2 t. baking powder
1/2 t. salt
5 T. chilled butter, diced
1/3 c. cinnamon baking chips

1/2 c. half-and-half
1/2 t. vanilla extract
1 egg, beaten
1/2 c. milk
1/2 c. turbinado sugar

In a large bowl, combine flour, sugar, baking powder and salt; whisk
well. Cut in butter with a pastry blender or 2 knives until mixture
resembles coarse meal. Add cinnamon chips; mix until combined. In a
separate bowl, whisk together half-and-half, vanilla and egg. Add
half-and-half mixture to flour mixture; stir just until moistened and a
soft dough forms. Turn dough out onto a lightly floured surface. With
floured hands, knead dough about 4 times, until all ingredients are well
mixed. Divide dough into 2 balls. Pat one ball into a 6-inch circle,
3/4-inch thick. Cut circle into 6 wedges. Repeat with second ball.
Arrange wedges on parchment paper-lined baking sheets. Brush each
wedge with 2 teaspoons milk; sprinkle with 2 teaspoons turbinado
sugar. Bake at 425 degrees for about 17 minutes, until golden. Serve
warm, or cool on a wire rack. Makes one dozen.

Share homemade scones with a friend.
Wrap scones in a tea towel and tuck
them into a basket along with some
packets of spiced tea. A sweet gift
that says "I'm thinking of you!"

Cindy's Cinnamon Swirl

Cindy Neel
Gooseberry Patch

So easy to make...perfect with coffee before setting off on a weekend day of antique shopping or leaf peeping!

1-1/2 c. all-purpose flour
2 envs. rapid-rise yeast
1/4 c. sugar
1/4 t. salt
1/4 c. butter, melted and slightly cooled

1 egg, beaten
2/3 c. milk
3 T. butter, softened
3/4 c. brown sugar, packed
1-1/2 t. cinnamon

In a bowl, mix flour, yeast, sugar and salt; stir in melted butter and egg. Heat milk until very warm, 120 to 130 degrees; add to mixture and stir well. Turn batter into an 8"x8" baking pan sprayed with non-stick vegetable spray. Cover and let rise for 10 minutes. In a small bowl, mix remaining ingredients with a fork. Sprinkle butter mixture evenly over batter; poke topping into batter with fingers or a wooden spoon handle. Place in a cold oven; set oven to 350 degrees. Bake for 25 to 30 minutes, until lightly golden and set in the center. Cool for 10 minutes. Drizzle with Icing; cut into squares. Makes 9 servings.

Icing:

1 c. powdered sugar
1 T. butter, melted

1/2 t. vanilla extract
1 to 2 T. milk

Combine all ingredients, adding milk to a drizzling consistency.

Try steaming eggnog, instead of milk, for cappuccino... sprinkle with pumpkin pie spice for a warm-you-to-your-toes breakfast treat!

Cinnamon-Pecan Pull-Aparts

Minnie Olson
Conewango Valley, NY

Talk about an easy, last-minute breakfast treat! This is one of our favorites...it's fun to make & take for a Sunday brunch.

3/4 c. chopped pecans
2/3 c. brown sugar, packed
1/2 c. butter, melted
1/2 c. sour cream

1 t. maple flavoring or
   vanilla extract
2 12-oz. tubes refrigerated
   cinnamon rolls

In a large bowl, combine all ingredients except cinnamon rolls; mix well. Separate rolls and cut each into quarters; set aside icing packet from rolls. Add roll pieces to pecan mixture; toss gently to coat. Spoon mixture into a greased tube pan. Bake at 350 degrees for 30 to 40 minutes, until deeply golden. Cool in pan for 10 minutes; invert onto a serving plate. Spread with reserved icing. Serve warm. Makes 12 servings.

Pancake breakfasts are a favorite small-town tradition, often held at a local elementary school, church or grange hall. Watch for announcements in your newspaper for this fun annual event.

Pumpkin Flax Muffins

Ginny Hale
Wasilla, AK

A tasty, healthful way to start the day! These muffins are perfect with a mug of hot cocoa on a crisp autumn morning.

1-1/2 c. bran flake cereal, crushed
1 c. whole-wheat flour
1/2 c. all-purpose flour
2 t. baking powder
1/2 t. baking soda
1/4 t. salt
2 t. pumpkin pie spice
1 t. cinnamon

1 egg, beaten
3/4 c. canned pumpkin
1 c. buttermilk
3/4 c. honey
1/4 c. olive oil
1/4 c. flax seed
1/2 c. pumpkin seeds
Optional: 1/2 c. chopped pecans

In a large bowl, mix together cereal, flours, baking powder, baking soda, salt and spices. In a separate bowl, combine remaining ingredients; stir well and add to cereal mixture. Mix well. Spoon batter into greased muffin cups, filling 2/3 full. Bake at 350 degrees for 12 to 15 minutes. Cool muffins in pan for 10 minutes before removing. Makes 1-1/2 dozen.

A big yellowware bowl is terrific for stirring up pancake and muffin batter. When not in use, fill it with shiny red apples to double as a casual harvest centerpiece.

Ginger Spice Muffins

Eleanor Dionne
Beverly, MA

Moist and golden, these muffins taste like gingerbread cupcakes!
Serve for breakfast or brunch with softened cream cheese.

1-1/4 c. all-purpose flour
1/4 c. sugar
1/2 t. baking soda
1/4 t. salt
1/2 t. cinnamon
1/2 t. ground ginger

1/8 t. nutmeg
1/2 c. light molasses
1/2 c. buttermilk
1/4 c. shortening
1 egg, beaten
1/2 c. chopped walnuts

In a large bowl, mix flour, sugar, baking soda, salt and spices. Add remaining ingredients. With an electric mixer on low speed, beat just until blended. Increase speed to medium and beat for 2 minutes. Spoon batter into greased or paper-lined muffin cups, filling 2/3 full. Bake at 375 degrees for 20 to 25 minutes. Cool in pan for 10 minutes; remove muffins to a wire rack and cool completely. Makes one dozen.

During the first week of school, deliver a tray of your favorite breakfast goodies to the teachers' lounge... it's sure to be appreciated!

Yummilicious Apple Muffins

Aubrey Nygren-Earl
Taylorsville, UT

The name of this recipe says it all! We love the added twist the almonds and cranberries give it. If you're not a fan of cranberries, just replace them with raisins.

2 c. all-purpose flour
1 c. sugar
2 t. baking powder
2 t. baking soda
2 t. cinnamon
1 t. nutmeg
2 eggs, beaten

1/2 c. unsweetened applesauce
5 c. Gala apples, peeled, cored and coarsely chopped
1 c. chopped almonds
1/2 c. sweetened dried cranberries

In a bowl, mix together flour, sugar, baking powder, baking soda and spices. In a separate bowl, whisk together eggs and applesauce. Fold in apples, almonds and cranberries; add to flour mixture and stir just until moistened. Spray muffin cups with non-stick vegetable spray. Fill muffin cups 2/3 full. Bake at 350 degrees for 20 minutes. Makes 2 dozen.

Call up your best girlfriends and enjoy shopping the day after Thanksgiving. Meet very early and share some scrumptious breakfast goodies to fortify yourselves, then head for the nearest small town to explore its little shops. Afterwards, invite everyone back for a leisurely lunch and talk about all the wonderful treasures you found.

Apricot-Pineapple Sunshine Bread *Sharon Demers*
Dolores, CO

After receiving an abundance of apricots and making two batches of jam, I was looking for a way to use them up. This tasty quick bread makes two loaves...nice to share with a neighbor!

3 eggs, beaten
1 c. oil
2 t. vanilla extract
1-1/2 c. apricots, peeled, pitted
    and chopped
1-1/2 c. crushed pineapple,
    drained
2 c. plus 2 T. sugar, divided

3 c. all-purpose flour
1 t. salt
1/2 t. baking powder
2 t. baking soda
2 t. cinnamon
Optional: 1 c. chopped walnuts
1/8 t. nutmeg

In a bowl, combine eggs, oil, vanilla, fruit and 2 cups sugar. In a separate large bowl, combine remaining ingredients except nutmeg and remaining sugar. Add egg mixture to flour mixture; stir until just combined. Pour batter evenly into two 9"x5" loaf pans sprayed with non-stick vegetable spray. Mix together nutmeg and remaining sugar. Sprinkle loaves lightly with sugar mixture. Bake at 350 degrees for 45 minutes to one hour. Cool 10 minutes in pans; turn out onto a wire rack and cool completely. Makes 2 loaves.

A new way to enjoy quick bread! Cut into thick slices and butter both sides. Grill or broil until golden and toasted. Sprinkle with powdered sugar and serve with fresh fruit...yummy!

Baked Fruit & Nut Oatmeal

Janet Reinhart
Columbia, IL

My husband Dan & I first tried this special dish at a B & B in Tennessee. It was served in a large bowl with ice cream on top! It's a very easy dish, with many variations, for family & friends over the holidays. For another way to enjoy it, omit the nuts and dried fruit. Serve topped with sliced fresh fruit and a little cream.

1 c. milk
2 eggs
1/4 c. oil
1 t. vanilla extract
1/2 c. brown sugar, packed
1-1/2 t. baking powder
1/2 t. salt

1 t. cinnamon
2 c. long-cooking oats, uncooked
Optional: 1/2 c. chopped almonds
Optional: 1/2 c. sweetened dried
   cranberries or raisins
Garnish: vanilla ice cream or
   yogurt

In a blender, combine milk, eggs, oil, vanilla, brown sugar, baking powder, salt and cinnamon. Process for about 30 seconds; pour into a large bowl. Stir in oats and optional ingredients, as desired. Let stand for 5 minutes. Pour into a greased 8"x8" glass baking pan. Bake, uncovered, at 325 degrees for 35 to 45 minutes. Serve warm, topped with a scoop of ice cream or yogurt. Serves 4 to 6.

Let the kids whip up some birdseed bagels so the birds can enjoy breakfast as the weather turns chilly. Just spread peanut butter on the cut side of a bagel; coat with birdseed. Slip a length of twine in the bagel hole and hang from a tree.

Scrumptious Baked Granola

Lisa Ann Panzino DiNunzio
Vineland, NJ

A super healthy and delicious way to start your day! Serve this granola topped with milk, or sprinkle over yogurt as a crunchy topping.

3 c. long-cooking oats, uncooked
3/4 c. chopped walnuts, pecans or almonds
1/2 c. maple syrup or agave nectar
1/4 c. safflower or sunflower oil
1/4 c. honey
1 T. wheat germ
Optional: 1 T. flax seed meal
1 t. cinnamon
1 t. vanilla extract
3/4 c. raisins, sweetened dried cranberries or cherries

In a large bowl, combine all ingredients except fruit; mix well. Spread on a 15"x10" jelly-roll pan sprayed with non-stick vegetable spray. Bake at 325 degrees for 25 to 35 minutes, stirring occasionally. Remove from oven; stir in fruit. Granola may still be sticky when it comes out of the oven, but will become crisp and dry as it cools. Let cool completely; store in airtight containers. Serves 6 to 8.

Such a neighborly gesture...invite the family of your child's new school friend over for a weekend brunch. Send them home with a basket filled with maps and coupons to local shops and attractions.

Breakfast Pumpkin Butter

JoAnn Ragland
Bedford, VA

*This is one of my mom's favorites...our family loves it year 'round.
It's a wonderful spread for toast and muffins. Spooned into a
canning jar, it makes an excellent hostess gift too!*

29-oz. can pumpkin
3/4 c. apple juice
1-1/2 c. sugar
2 t. ground ginger

2 t. ground cinnamon
1 t. nutmeg
1/2 t. ground cloves

Combine all ingredients in a large saucepan; stir well. Bring to a boil
over medium heat; reduce heat to low. Simmer for about 30 minutes,
stirring frequently, until thickened. Transfer to containers; cover and
keep refrigerated. Makes about 3 cups.

Honey-Pecan Butter

Barb Bargdill
Gooseberry Patch

This spread is really yummy on warm cornbread!

1 lb. butter, room temperature
1/2 c. pecan halves

1/4 c. honey

Place butter in a large bowl; set aside. Arrange pecans on an ungreased
baking sheet. Bake at 350 degrees until toasted, 5 to 8 minutes. Let
cool; chop and add to butter. Beat mixture with an electric mixer on
medium-high speed for 3 to 5 minutes. Add honey; continue to beat
until well combined. Place in a serving bowl; cover and keep
refrigerated. Makes about 2 cups.

Make an easy fabric liner for a gift basket of jam and fresh-baked
muffins. With pinking shears, cut a big square of cotton fabric in
a perky fall print. Scraps can be used for cute jar toppers.

CHURCH SOCIAL
Soup Supper

Fried Corn Chowder

Ruby Pruitt
Nashville, IN

One day I gave my mom some fresh corn on the cob, and she said she would take it home and make fried corn. That gave me the idea for this yummy recipe. My easy Beer Bread goes really well with this chowder.

3 T. butter, divided
2 c. fresh or frozen corn
2 T. dried, minced onion
2 c. potatoes, peeled and finely
   diced

2 c. hot water
2 T. all-purpose flour
2 c. milk
1 t. salt
1/8 t. pepper

Melt one tablespoon butter in a saucepan over low heat. Add corn; cook, stirring often, until tender. Meanwhile, melt remaining butter in a separate large saucepan. Add onion and cook until lightly golden, stirring often. Add potatoes and hot water. Simmer until potatoes are tender. Drain half of the liquid. In a bowl, add flour to milk; whisk until no lumps are visible. Add salt and pepper. Stir flour mixture into hot potato mixture; blend well and stir in corn. Simmer until flavors are blended, about 10 minutes. Serve hot with Beer Bread. Makes 6 to 8 servings.

Beer Bread:

3 c. all-purpose flour
1/4 c. sugar
1 T. baking powder
1 t. salt

12-oz. can beer or non-alcoholic
   beer
2 T. butter, melted

In a bowl, stir together flour, sugar, baking powder and salt. Add beer; mix well. Pour into a greased 9"x5" loaf pan. Drizzle butter on top. Bake at 375 degrees for about 40 to 50 minutes, until golden. Slice while still warm. Makes one loaf.

Little sugar pumpkins are sweet
soup bowls...the ideal size!

Yummy Bean & Tortellini Soup
Gloria Morris
British Columbia, Canada

One of my best friends made a similar soup when we traveled to visit her. Although she has since passed away, I conjured up this recipe that's really yummy, quick to make and filling. Good with fresh-baked biscuits for a chilly evening.

1 lb. ground Italian pork sausage
2 15-oz. cans garbanzo beans,
    drained
6-oz. can tomato paste
4 c. water
1 c. sliced mushrooms

1 c. onion, sliced
1/4 t. dried marjoram
1 t. salt
1 t. pepper
16-oz. pkg. refrigerated or dried
    cheese tortellini, uncooked

Form sausage into marble-size balls; add to a large Dutch oven or soup pot. Cook over medium-high heat until browned; drain. Stir in remaining ingredients. Simmer over medium-low heat for about 30 minutes, stirring occasionally, until tortellini is tender. Serves 4.

Stitch up a simple fleece block quilt in school colors to cozy up under for nighttime football games. For extra chilly nights, make a matching drawstring bag and tuck a hot water bottle inside.

Garden-Fresh Chili

Caroline Timbs
Batesville, AR

My husband and I concocted this recipe to use our own garden-fresh canned tomatoes and home-grown green peppers from our freezer. Sometimes I like to add a small can of tomato sauce. If you prefer your chili with beans, just add a can or two of kidney beans.

2-1/2 lbs. ground beef
1 onion, chopped
1 green pepper, chopped
4 c. home-canned tomatoes,
   or 2 to 3 14-1/2 oz. cans
   whole tomatoes

2 1-1/4 oz. pkgs. chili
   seasoning mix
6 T. water
Garnish: shredded cheese,
   cornbread or corn chips

In a large stockpot over medium heat, cook beef, onion and green pepper; drain. Stir in tomatoes with juice; mash tomatoes until well blended. Add seasoning mix and water; stir until mixed. Bring to a boil; reduce heat to low. Cover and simmer for one hour, stirring occasionally. Garnish bowls of chili with cheese. Serve with cornbread or corn chips. Makes 6 to 8 servings.

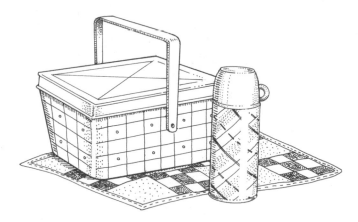

On a crisp autumn afternoon, load up a thermos with chili and toss in some lunch-size bags of corn chips, shredded Cheddar cheese and spoons. Take a hike in the woods, then enjoy a portable picnic of chili ladled over the chips and eaten right from the bags. Kids will love it!

CHURCH SOCIAL
Soup Supper

Spicy Meatball Noodle Soup

Jonni Sue Wilhelm
Hebron, MD

This recipe is one I've been using and improving on for ages. We love spicy foods and like to try to be healthier, so I have added more & more whole-wheat pasta to it over the years.

6 14-1/2 oz. cans chicken broth
3 10-oz. cans diced tomatoes
    with green chiles
4-1/2 t. garlic, minced and
    divided
1 T. ground cumin
1-1/2 lbs. lean ground beef
3 c. shredded Mexican-blend
    cheese, divided

1 t. salt
1 t. pepper
8-oz. pkg. fettuccine pasta,
    uncooked
8-oz. pkg. whole-wheat linguine
    pasta, divided
3 zucchini, diced

In a large soup pot, combine broth, tomatoes with juice, 3 teaspoons garlic and cumin. Bring to a boil over medium-high heat. Reduce heat to low; cover and simmer for 10 minutes. Meanwhile, in a bowl, combine beef, remaining garlic, 1-1/2 cups cheese, salt and pepper. Form into 3/4-inch meatballs; add meatballs to broth mixture. Cover and cook for 5 minutes. Break fettuccine and half of linguine into 2-inch pieces; reserve remaining linguine for use in another recipe. Add broken pasta and zucchini to soup pot. Return to a boil; cook until pasta is tender, about 10 minutes. Serve soup topped with remaining cheese. Makes 10 to 12 servings.

Be sure to stop at roadside stands in the country. You'll find pumpkins with fun names like Cinderella, Big Max and Baby Boo, as well as gourds in all sizes, shapes and colors. Pick up everything you need for fall decorating!

Howdy to Harvest Soup

Delaney Rannells
Omaha, NE

*This delicious, veggie-packed recipe is the best way
to welcome your family into fall!*

1 T. olive oil
1-1/2 c. onion, chopped
2 carrots, peeled and chopped
2 stalks celery, chopped
4 cloves garlic, minced
1/2 t. dried basil
1/2 t. dried thyme
4 c. low-sodium vegetable broth
4 c. water
2 14-1/2 oz. cans diced tomatoes

3/4 lb. sweet potato, peeled and
  diced
1/2 lb. potatoes, peeled and diced
1/2 lb. green beans, cut into
  1-inch pieces
2 15-oz. cans white beans,
  drained and rinsed
1/2 lb. fresh kale, chopped
Garnish: grated Parmesan cheese

In a large soup pot, heat oil over medium-high heat. Add onion, carrots,
celery, garlic and herbs. Cook, stirring occasionally, for about 7 minutes,
or until vegetables are soft. Add broth, water, tomatoes with juice and
potatoes; bring to a boil. Reduce heat to low; cover and simmer for
15 minutes. Stir in beans and kale; simmer another 15 minutes. Garnish
soup bowls with cheese. Serves 6.

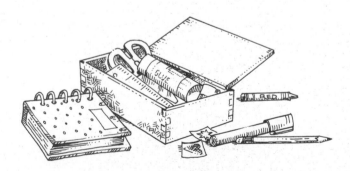

In early autumn, before the busy holiday season begins,
why not invite friends to a crafting get-together? Choose a
simple craft like ornaments or package tie-ons. You provide craft
materials, a work table and a beverage...guests bring a goodie
to share. Everyone is sure to have a wonderful time!

40

Miss Kelli's Corn Cakes

Kelli Venable
Ostrander, OH

These are so good! My grandma gave me some cornmeal and I used it in this recipe. I like blueberries, so sometimes I'll add 1/2 cup of berries to the batter...yum!

1-1/4 c. all-purpose flour
1/3 c. sugar
3/4 c. yellow cornmeal
2 t. baking powder

1/2 t. salt
3/4 c. milk
1/4 c. oil
1 to 2 egg whites, beaten

In a large bowl, mix flour, sugar, cornmeal, baking powder and salt. Make a well in the center. In a small bowl, whisk together milk, oil and egg; pour into well in flour mixture and stir until well blended. Coat a large skillet with non-stick vegetable spray; heat over medium heat. Add batter by 1/4 cupfuls. Cook for 2 minutes on each side, flattening with a pancake turner to cook through to the center. If necessary, spray skillet again when adding more batter. Makes 6 to 9 servings.

Cloverleaf Rolls

Eleanor Howell
Falmouth, ME

I used to make yeast rolls for Thanksgiving, then I spotted the frozen bread dough at the supermarket and thought, why not try to make rolls out of it? Now I get all the praise with very little mess!

1 loaf frozen bread dough, thawed

Garnish: softened butter

Spray a muffin tin with non-stick vegetable spray; set aside. Pull dough apart into 1/2-inch balls. Place 3 dough balls in each muffin cup; spread butter on top. Cover and let rise for 3 hours. Bake at 350 degrees for 20 minutes, or until golden. Makes about one dozen.

Keep freshly baked bread warm and toasty...simply slip a piece of aluminum foil into a bread basket, then top it with a decorative napkin.

Skinny Pumpkin Soup

Jenn Erickson
Pacific Grove, CA

Last October I felt like I was beginning to look a bit too much like a pumpkin myself, so I decided to slim down my traditional pumpkin soup recipe without sacrificing its flavor. A healthy alternative that tastes terrific is cause for celebration!

1 lb. sweet potatoes, halved
   lengthwise
1 T. butter
2 shallots, sliced
4 cloves garlic, pressed
6 c. chicken or vegetable broth
15-oz. can pumpkin
1 t. ground ginger

1/4 t. cinnamon
1/4 t. allspice
1/4 t. nutmeg
1 t. salt, plus more to taste
1/2 c. evaporated milk
3 T. honey
pepper to taste
Garnish: low-fat sour cream

Spray sweet potatoes on both sides with non-stick vegetable spray. Place on a baking sheet, cut-side down. Bake at 350 degrees for one hour, or until fork-tender. When cool enough to handle, scoop out potato pulp and set aside; discard skins. Melt butter in a large Dutch oven over medium-high heat. Add shallots and garlic; sauté until shallots are translucent and garlic is golden. Add sweet potatoes to mixture in Dutch oven, breaking up potatoes as you stir. Add broth; whisk to combine. Whisk in pumpkin, spices and salt. Bring to a simmer. Simmer, uncovered, over medium-low for 15 minutes, whisking occasionally to prevent scorching. Reduce heat to low. With a stick blender, or transferring soup to a blender, process soup until smooth. Stir in milk and honey; simmer over low heat for 5 more minutes. Season with salt and pepper. Serve garnished with a dollop of sour cream. Serves 8.

A terrific getaway on a sunny fall day! Check out some nearby places you've always wanted to see...gardens, craft shops, historic houses. Pack a picnic lunch and stop at a park you've never visited before.

Hearty Healthy Potato Soup

Carolyn Deckard
Bedford, IN

A wonderful soup to make on brisk autumn days.

6 potatoes, peeled and sliced
2 carrots, peeled and diced
6 stalks celery, diced
8 c. water
1 onion, chopped
6 T. light margarine

6 T. all-purpose flour
1 t. salt
1/2 t. pepper
1-1/2 c. reduced-fat milk
fat-free saltine crackers

In a stockpot over medium heat, combine potatoes, carrots, celery and water. Cook until vegetables are tender, 30 to 40 minutes. Drain, reserving liquid and setting vegetables aside. In the same stockpot, sauté onion in margarine until soft. Stir in flour, salt and pepper. Gradually add milk; cook and stir until thickened, about 5 minutes. Stir in cooked vegetables carefully so as not to mash them. Add one cup or more of reserved cooking liquid until soup reaches the desired consistency. Serve with crackers. Makes 8 servings.

A soup supper in front of a crackling fire...how cozy! Invite friends to bring their favorite veggies and cook up a big pot of hearty vegetable soup together. While the soup simmers, you can catch up on conversation.

Famous Clam Chowder

Jacque Zehner
Modesto, CA

I've been making this chowder longer than I can remember...I don't even remember where I got the recipe! Everyone loves it, so I usually double the recipe. Good with French or sourdough bread.

2 c. potatoes, peeled and finely
    diced
1 c. onion, finely chopped
1 c. celery, finely diced
6-1/2 oz. can minced clams,
    drained and juice reserved
3/4 c. butter

3/4 c. all-purpose flour
1 qt. half-and-half
2 T. red wine vinegar
1-1/2 t. salt
pepper to taste
Optional: crisply cooked,
    crumbled bacon

Combine vegetables and reserved clam juice in a large saucepan. Add enough water to barely cover vegetables. Cover and simmer over medium heat until just tender, about 20 minutes. Meanwhile, melt butter in a separate large saucepan over medium heat. Add flour; cook and stir for 2 to 3 minutes. Add half-and-half; cook and stir with a whisk until smooth and thick. Remove from heat. Add clams and undrained vegetables to half-and-half mixture; heat through. Add vinegar, salt and pepper; mix well. Sprinkle with bacon, if desired. Chowder will thicken if refrigerated; thin with more milk or water when reheating. Makes about 8 servings.

Use mini cookie cutters to cut bread into whimsical soup croutons...tiny leaves make a harvest dinner fun. Brush cutouts with olive oil and a sprinkling of herbs. Bake at 200 degrees for about 10 minutes, until croutons are golden.

CHURCH SOCIAL
Soup Supper

Debbie's Clam Fritters

Debra Jurczyk
Gilbertville, MA

Years ago, we used to have clambakes in our area where you bought a ticket and went for the whole day, with terrific food and company, even a live band for dancing. They served these wonderful fritters to go with the clam chowder. When the clambakes ended and no one knew how to make the fritters, I decided to create my own. They have been a hit ever since. I even made them at a campground in Rhode Island... the campground owners asked for my recipe so they could use it at their restaurant!

16-oz. can shortening
1-1/2 c. all-purpose flour
1 T. baking powder
3/4 t. salt

1 egg, beaten
1 c. clam broth
1 c. chopped clams

Melt shortening in a large deep pot. Place a frying thermometer on the edge of the pot and heat to 375 degrees, watching thermometer carefully to avoid burning. Meanwhile, in a small bowl, mix flour, baking powder and salt. In a separate large bowl, whisk together egg and clam broth; add clams and mix well. Add flour mixture; stir just until moistened. Drop batter into hot shortening by high rounded teaspoonfuls, about 12 at a time. Fry about 3 to 4 minutes, turning as fritters turn golden. Drain on a large tray lined with paper towels. Serve hot. Makes 2 dozen.

Whip up some fresh corn fritters. Follow the recipe for
Debbie's Clam Fritters, but use corn kernels instead of clams
and milk instead of clam broth. Serve with maple syrup
for dipping...yummy!

Black Kettle Brunswick Stew

Cyndi Little
Whitsett, NC

From my childhood, I can remember a woman stirring this stew in a black kettle in her yard. You can imagine what I was thinking! Fortunately she wasn't the neighborhood witch, as others said to scare the little kids, but a kind woman making good stew for her family. So delicious on a fall evening! For extra richness, use chicken broth instead of water.

3 to 5 lbs. boneless, skinless
    chicken, cubed
3 to 5 lbs. stew beef cubes
8 c. potatoes, peeled and diced
12 c. tomatoes, chopped
4 c. onion, chopped
4 c. corn
4 c. peas
2 c. carrots, peeled and diced

2 T. sugar
1/4 c. Worcestershire sauce
1/2 c. vinegar
1/2 c. catsup
2 dried red chiles, or hot pepper
    sauce to taste
salt and pepper to taste
Garnish: saltine crackers

Place chicken and beef in a 4-gallon stockpot; add water to cover. Bring to a boil over medium heat; reduce to low and simmer until tender. Remove meat from pot, reserving cooking liquid. Allow meat to cool; pull apart into bite-size pieces. Add potatoes and carrots to reserved cooking liquid; cook just until tender. Add remaining ingredients except crackers; return meat to stockpot. Simmer over low heat for 3 to 4 hours, until stew thickens. Stir occasionally to prevent sticking. Serve with crackers. Makes 24 servings.

Pitch a tent in the backyard on a fall
night so the kids can camp out, tell
ghost stories and play flashlight tag.
What a way to make memories!

Vegetable Soup for a Crowd

Janice Reinhardt
Bethel Park, PA

I love homemade soup...there's nothing more comforting than a hot bowl of soup to warm you on a chilly day! This recipe feeds a large group. You can adjust the amount of vegetables to your liking, and stew beef may also be added.

3 T. butter
4 to 5 c. cabbage, chopped
1 onion, chopped
3 carrots, peeled and chopped
3 32-oz. containers chicken
    broth, divided
3 potatoes, peeled and diced

4 stalks celery, chopped
2 14-1/2 oz. cans diced tomatoes
salt and pepper to taste
2 bay leaves
15-oz. can cut green beans,
    drained
15-oz. can corn, drained

Melt butter in a large stockpot over medium-low heat. Add cabbage, onion, carrots and just enough chicken broth to cover. Cover and bring to a boil. Reduce heat to low; simmer for about 20 minutes, stirring often. Add remaining broth, potatoes, celery, tomatoes with juice and seasonings. Increase heat to high; cover and bring to a boil. Reduce heat; simmer for an additional 30 minutes, or until vegetables are soft. About 5 minutes before serving time, stir in beans and corn; heat through. Discard bay leaves; add more salt and pepper, as needed. Serves 18 to 20.

We all have hometown appetites.
—Clementine Paddleford

Chicken & Wild Rice Soup ▶

Emily Martin
Ontario, Canada

Delicious, satisfying and good enough for company!

3 14-oz. cans chicken broth,
    divided
1 c. carrots, peeled and coarsely
    chopped
1/2 c. celery, chopped
1/2 c. onion, chopped
2 c. sliced mushrooms
1/2 c. wild rice, uncooked

2 T. butter
1/4 c. all-purpose flour
4 t. salt
1/4 t. pepper
1 c. whipping cream
2 c. cooked chicken, diced
Optional: sour cream, snipped
    fresh chives

In a Dutch oven over medium heat, combine 2 cans broth, carrots, celery, onion, mushrooms and rice. Bring to a boil; reduce heat to low. Cover and simmer for 35 to 40 minutes, until rice is nearly tender. In a separate saucepan, melt butter over medium heat. Stir in flour, salt and pepper; add remaining broth. Cook and stir until thickened and bubbly; continue stirring for one more minute. Stir in whipping cream. Stirring constantly, add cream mixture to rice mixture. Add chicken; heat through. Garnish soup bowls with dollops of sour cream and chopped chives, if desired. Serves 8.

If frost is in the forecast, you can still save the herbs in
the garden! Spoon chopped fresh herbs into an ice cube tray,
one tablespoon per cube. Cover with water and freeze.
Frozen cubes can be dropped right into hot soups
or stews for a pop of fresh flavor.

Day-After-Thanksgiving Soup   *JoAnn*

*With a big scoop of dressing in each bowl, this yummy soup
is hearty enough to get you through a day of Black Friday
shopping or decorating for Christmas.*

1 T. olive oil
2 carrots, peeled and chopped
2 stalks celery, chopped
1 onion, chopped
salt and pepper to taste
8 c. turkey or chicken broth

1 bay leaf
1-1/2 c. roast turkey, diced
1 c. frozen peas
2 T. fresh parsley, chopped
4 to 6 c. leftover dressing,
    warmed

Heat oil in a large stockpot over medium heat. Add carrots, celery,
onion, salt and pepper. Sauté until vegetables are crisp-tender. Add
broth and bay leaf; bring to a boil. Stir in turkey; reduce heat and
simmer for about 10 minutes, until vegetables are tender. Stir in peas
and parsley; warm through. Discard bay leaf. To serve, place a scoop of
dressing into individual deep soup bowls. Ladle soup over dressing.
Serves 4 to 6.

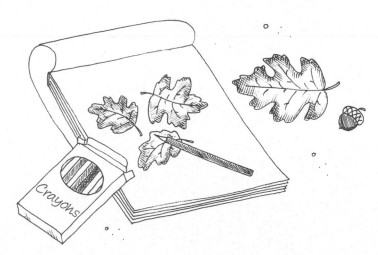

Make some autumn placemats with leaf rubbings...fun for kids!
Arrange leaves face-down on plain white paper and cover with
another sheet of paper. Remove wrappers from crayons and
rub over the leaves. Their images will magically appear.

Willie Family Chili

Susan Willie
Ridgecrest, NC

*My husband Stephen created this recipe several
years ago...now it's a family favorite.*

2 lbs. ground beef
1/2 to 1 c. onion, chopped
2 15-oz. cans pinto beans
28-oz. can diced tomatoes
15-oz. can tomato sauce
6-oz. can tomato paste

1 c. water
2 T. chili powder
1/2 t. dried oregano
1/2 t. salt
1/2 t. pepper

Brown beef in a soup pot over medium heat; drain. Stir in remaining
ingredients. Bring to a boil. Reduce heat to low; cover and simmer for
one hour. For best flavor, refrigerate overnight, then reheat and serve
the following day. Makes 8 to 10 servings.

Sesame Skillet Bread

Chad Rutan
Gooseberry Patch

Easy to stir up...just right with a bowl of hot soup!

1-1/3 c. cornmeal
2/3 c. whole-wheat flour
2 t. baking powder
1 t. salt
1/4 c. wheat germ

2 T. sesame seed
1-3/4 c. milk
3 T. oil
1 egg, beaten

In a bowl, stir together cornmeal, flour, baking powder, salt, wheat
germ and sesame seed. Add milk, oil and egg; stir until moistened.
Spoon into a greased 9" cast-iron skillet. Bake at 400 degrees for 25 to
30 minutes. Cut into wedges; serve warm. Serves 8.

Place the dry ingredients for Sesame Skillet Bread in a muslin
bag and tuck into a cast-iron skillet for a gift that's sure
to be enjoyed. Be sure to tie on a recipe card!

Sausage & Kale Soup

Diana Clarcq
Richmond, VA

My wonderful husband Jim took care of me while I was sick, so I wanted to do something special for him. I decided to make my own version of a soup he'd enjoyed at a restaurant. When he tasted the soup, he was so excited! He said I had outdone myself. I was so pleased I could do this for him. We still make this soup every winter...it has become one of our favorites.

16-oz. pkg. apple-stuffed chicken
    sausage links, casings
    removed
2 t. olive oil
3 32-oz. containers chicken
    broth
4 redskin potatoes, peeled and
    diced

1 sweet onion, diced
2 T. fresh basil, snipped
1 t. salt
1 to 1-1/2 t. pepper
1 bunch fresh kale, chopped
1 c. whipping cream

In a skillet over medium heat, cook sausage in oil, breaking it up into small pieces; drain. Add broth to a soup pot; bring to a boil over medium heat. Add potatoes, onion, basil and seasonings to broth. Cook until potatoes are tender, 10 to 15 minutes. Stir in sausage and kale. Cook over very low heat until kale wilts slightly. Whisk in cream; simmer for 10 to 15 minutes. Makes 4 servings.

Begin a new and heartfelt Thanksgiving tradition. Ask your family & friends to bring a pair of warm mittens or gloves to dinner, then deliver them to your local shelter.

Tortellini Caprese Soup

Lisa Engwell
Bellevue, NE

*Put this comforting soup together quickly on chilly nights
when you're pressed for time!*

32-oz. container chicken broth
14-1/2 oz. can diced tomatoes
  with basil, garlic and oregano
Optional: 1 T. garlic, minced
9-oz. pkg. refrigerated 3-cheese
  tortellini, uncooked

Garnish: shredded mozzarella
  cheese, snipped fresh basil,
  garlic croutons

In a large saucepan, combine broth, tomatoes with juice and garlic, if using. Bring to a boil over medium heat. Add pasta and cook according to package directions. Garnish as desired. Serves 4.

Cracked Pepper Bread Sticks

Jackie Smulski
Lyons, IL

*Homemade bread sticks coming right up! Adjust the amount
of pepper to your own taste.*

2 c. all-purpose flour
1 T. baking powder
1/4 t. salt

1 to 1-1/2 t. cracked pepper
1/3 c. butter
2/3 c. beef broth

In a bowl, stir together flour, baking powder, salt and pepper. Cut in butter with a fork until mixture resembles coarse crumbs. Make a well in the center. Pour broth into well; stir lightly until moistened. On a floured surface, knead dough gently for 10 to 12 strokes. Divide dough into 8 portions; divide each portion into quarters. Roll each piece into a 10-inch rope; twist. Arrange twists on ungreased baking sheets. Bake at 425 degrees for 5 minutes; turn over. Bake for an additional 5 to 6 minutes, until light golden. Serve warm, or cool on a wire rack. Makes about 2-1/2 dozen.

Freezer Onion Soup

Sandra Sullivan
Aurora, CO

I use my home-grown onions in this recipe. We take jars of this soup
to ski buddies over the holidays. It tastes so good after a day on
the slopes...who wouldn't love to receive a jar of savory soup?

2 lbs. onions, sliced
6 T. butter
1 t. sugar
1 t. dry mustard
3 T. all-purpose flour

8 c. beef broth
1 c. dry sherry or beef broth
salt and pepper to taste
Optional: croutons, shredded
    Swiss cheese

In a heavy saucepan over medium heat, cook onions in butter until
transparent and golden. Add sugar and mustard. Blend in flour;
gradually stir in beef broth and sherry or broth. Simmer for 30 minutes.
Season with salt and pepper. Cool; ladle into freezer-safe containers,
leaving 1/2-inch headspace. Seal containers and freeze for up to
2 months. Thaw and reheat to serve. If desired, ladle into individual
oven-proof bowls; top with croutons and cheese. Broil for 2 to
3 minutes, until cheese is melted. Makes about 8 servings.

Lacy cheese crisps are delicious
soup toppers. For each crisp, sprinkle
2 tablespoons shredded Parmesan
cheese, 4 inches apart, onto a baking
sheet lined with a silicone baking
mat. Bake at 400 degrees for 6 to
8 minutes, until golden. Cool
slightly and add to soup bowls.

Autumn Vegetable Soup

Mary Lou Savage
McKeesport, PA

*I always liked to make this soup on crisp autumn afternoons
for when my kids arrived home from school. I served it with
homemade bread & butter...they loved it!*

1 lb. ground beef
1 c. onion, diced
4 c. hot water
1 c. carrots, peeled and diced
1 c. celery, diced
1 c. potatoes, peeled and diced

1 bay leaf
1/8 t. dried basil
2 t. salt
1/2 t. pepper
1 cube beef bouillon
6 tomatoes, chopped

In a Dutch oven over medium heat, cook beef until browned. Add onion
and cook for 5 minutes; drain. Add remaining ingredients except
tomatoes. Bring to a boil; reduce heat to low. Cover and simmer for
20 to 25 minutes. Add tomatoes and simmer for 10 to 15 minutes
longer. Remove bay leaf before serving. Serves 6.

For a real hometown feel, make the most of your front porch!
A porch swing, rocking chairs, comfy pillows and hanging baskets
of fall flowers create a cozy place for family & friends to visit
and enjoy the crisp air.

Chicken Pot Pie Soup

*Carrie Allen
Dillon, CO*

*This soup smells and tastes like fall to me! I love to make it on cool
days to warm up my family. You can also thicken the soup a little
more and top with a crust for a delicious chicken pot pie.*

2 c. potatoes, peeled and cubed
1 c. carrots, peeled and sliced
1 c. frozen petite green peas
6 T. butter, sliced
1/3 c. all-purpose flour

4 c. whole milk
5 t. chicken bouillon granules
1/4 t. pepper
2 c. cooked chicken, cubed

In a soup pot, cover potatoes and carrots with water. Cook over
medium-high heat until tender, 10 to 15 minutes. Add peas; cook until
tender, 3 to 5 minutes. Drain; set vegetables aside in a bowl. In the
same pot, melt butter over medium heat. Stir in flour; cook and stir
until mixture is golden. Add milk, bouillon and pepper to butter mixture.
Cook and stir over medium heat until thickened. Add chicken and
vegetables; heat through. Makes 5 to 6 servings.

Crisp fall weather, antiquing and picnicking seem to go together.
Take time from after a day of treasure-hunting with friends to
enjoy a packable feast. Keep it simple...sandwiches, thermoses
of soup and cookies to nibble on will be plenty.

Spinach Salad & Maple Vinaigrette
Andrea Heyart
Aubrey, TX

A perfect salad for Thanksgiving dinner or any cool-weather meal.

8 c. fresh baby spinach
2 tart green apples, cored and
   thinly sliced
1/2 c. sweetened dried
   cranberries

1/2 c. bacon, crisply cooked and
   crumbled
1/3 c. green onions, diced
1/2 c. crumbled blue cheese

Combine spinach, apples, cranberries, bacon and onions in a large salad bowl. Just before serving, drizzle with Maple Vinaigrette; toss to mix and top with crumbled blue cheese. Makes 8 servings.

Maple Vinaigrette:

1 c. olive oil
2/3 c. cider vinegar
1/2 c. maple syrup

2 t. Dijon mustard
1 T. orange juice
salt and pepper to taste

Whisk together all ingredients.

Add the taste of autumn to a favorite salad with a
quick toss of crunchy pumpkin seeds.

Honey-Ginger Wild Rice Salad

Jackie Flaherty
Saint Paul, MN

Wild rice is traditionally harvested in Minnesota in late August through September. We go to the farmers' market here in Saint Paul and buy a year's supply when it's freshly harvested. No matter the weather, as soon as this is done, it's officially autumn at our house!

3 c. cooked wild rice
1 to 2 bunches green onions,
   sliced
1 c. sweetened dried cranberries

1 c. red pepper, diced
1/2 c. salted roasted sunflower
   kernels
3/4 c. pine nuts

Combine all ingredients except pine nuts in a large salad bowl; toss to mix and set aside. Toast pine nuts in a dry skillet over medium-high heat, stirring until fragrant. Cool slightly and add to salad. Drizzle with Honey-Ginger Dressing; stir thoroughly to combine. Cover and refrigerate until serving time. Serves 8 to 10.

Honey-Ginger Dressing:

2 T. frozen orange juice
   concentrate
2 T. honey
2 T. toasted sesame oil

1 T. rice vinegar
1 T. soy sauce
1 to 2 T. fresh ginger, peeled
   and grated

Whisk together all ingredients, adding ginger to taste.

Greet visitors with a charming homespun wreath on the door. Simply tear checked homespun fabric in golds and browns into strips and tie onto a grapevine wreath.

Layered Asian Chicken Salad

Vickie

*Bored with the same old chicken salad? Asian flavors
and crunchy noodles really jazz it up!*

2 boneless, skinless chicken
  breasts, cooked and shredded
2/3 c. General Tso's sauce
1/4 c. teriyaki sauce
3 c. romaine lettuce, coarsely
  chopped
1 c. red cabbage, coarsely
  chopped

1/2 c. carrot, peeled and
  shredded
1/4 c. sliced almonds
2 T. chow mein noodles
1/4 c. green onions, sliced

Combine chicken and sauces in a skillet over medium-low heat. Cook
and stir until warmed through; remove from heat and let cool. In a clear
glass bowl, layer romaine, cabbage, carrot, almonds and noodles. Top
with chicken mixture and green onions. Serves 4.

Packing lunchboxes or picnic baskets? Tuck in a few homemade
ice packs. Soak clean new sponges in water, seal well in
small plastic zipping bags and freeze. So easy, and sponges
can be re-frozen many times.

Grandma Sue's Shrimp Salad

Kathy McNeilly
Dewitt, MI

As a little girl growing up in the 50's and 60's, I always looked forward to the holidays and Grandma Sue's Shrimp Salad. Grandma didn't measure, so my mother and I had to figure out the recipe. It has been run through our "test kitchen" until it's perfect. Make it the day before so it can marinate and will taste even better.

16-oz. pkg. small shell macaroni, uncooked
1 to 1-1/2 lbs. frozen cooked and peeled shrimp, thawed and patted dry
1 doz. eggs, hard-boiled, peeled and divided
1 c. celery, diced
2 c. mayonnaise-type salad dressing
1/4 c. milk
2-1/2 T. mustard
2 t. onion, minced
1-1/2 t. celery salt
3/4 t. salt
Garnish: paprika

Cook macaroni according to package directions; rinse with cold water. Drain; place in a large serving bowl. Cut shrimp into bite-size pieces and add to macaroni. Coarsely chop 10 eggs and add to macaroni mixture along with celery. In a small bowl, mix together salad dressing, milk, mustard, onion and salts. Add to macaroni mixture and stir well. Slice remaining eggs and arrange on top; lightly sprinkle with paprika. Cover and refrigerate until serving. May be made a day ahead of time. Serves 12 to 15.

The frost is on the pumpkin! For an elegant yet easy fall centerpiece, spray a pumpkin lightly with spray adhesive and sprinkle with clear glitter. Set the pumpkin on a cake stand and cover with a clear glass dome.

Best Pennsylvania Dutch Potato Salad

Bethi Hendrickson
Danville, PA

Our family lived away from home while my husband Brian served in the Army. Whenever I felt homesick for central Pennsylvania, I would make this yummy potato salad. It was always a fantastic addition to our evening supper and made me feel a little closer to our hometown.

6 to 8 potatoes, peeled and cubed
1 lb. bacon, crisply cooked,
    crumbled and 2 T. drippings
    reserved
2 eggs, beaten
1 c. milk
1 c. water

3/4 c. vinegar
3/4 c. sugar or calorie-free
    powdered sweetener
3 T. all-purpose flour
1/8 t. pepper
3 stalks celery, diced
Garnish: chopped fresh parsley

Cover potatoes with water in a stockpot. Cook over medium heat until tender, about 15 minutes; drain. Immediately run cold water over potatoes; cool and set aside. In a blender, combine bacon, reserved drippings and remaining ingredients except celery and garnish. Process until well mixed; pour into a saucepan. Cook over medium heat until thickened and bubbly, whisking frequently. Combine potatoes and celery. Pour hot mixture over top and toss to mix. Cover and refrigerate for several hours before serving. Garnish with parsley. Serves 8 to 10.

Thanksgiving Day is a fine time to get caught up with family & friends. Set up a memory table and have everybody bring along snapshots, clippings, even Susie's soccer trophy and Uncle Bob's latest travel photos...you'll all have plenty to talk about over dinner.

Incredible Roasted Sweet Potato Salad

Becky Drees
Pittsfield, MA

I first tasted this salad at a gathering. Just about everyone asked the woman who'd brought it for her recipe...that's how good it is!

3 lbs. sweet potatoes, peeled and
    cut into 1-inch cubes
2 T. olive oil
1 T. toasted sesame oil
1 T. ground cumin

salt and pepper to taste
3 c. seedless green grapes
1 c. sweetened dried cranberries
1 c. toasted almonds, coarsely
    chopped

In a bowl, combine sweet potatoes, oils and seasonings; toss to coat. Spread sweet potatoes on a baking sheet sprayed with non-stick vegetable spray. Bake at 375 degrees for one hour, or until tender and golden, stirring occasionally. Cool to room temperature. Transfer sweet potatoes to a large serving bowl; carefully fold in grapes, cranberries and almonds. Add Dressing and toss to coat. Serves 8 to 10.

Dressing:

1/4 c. olive oil
2-1/2 T. cider vinegar
2 T. maple syrup

1 T. curry powder
1 t. Dijon mustard

Whisk together all ingredients.

Dress up table settings in a snap...tuck a sprig of fragrant
herbs into each napkin ring.

Turkey Delight Sandwich

Miriam Ankerbrand
Greencastle, PA

A very simple sandwich, but filled with flavor! We used to enjoy a similar sandwich at a local restaurant...they served it on their fresh-baked bread with a side of potato chips in an old pie tin. Since the restaurant closed, we make the sandwich at home, but fondly remember the aroma of their bread.

1/2 c. jellied cranberry sauce
8 slices whole-grain bread

8 thick slices roast turkey
1/2 c. cream cheese, softened

Spread cranberry sauce over 4 bread slices; top each with 2 slices of turkey. Spread remaining slices with cream cheese; place on top of turkey. Cut in half and serve. Makes 4 servings.

Broiled Hamburger Sandwich

Terese Podolske
Las Vegas, NV

With seven kids in our family, my mother could whip up a platter of these open-faced cheeseburgers in no time on brisk autumn nights. She served them alongside cups of hot soup...so good!

1 lb. lean ground beef
8-oz. pkg. shredded Cheddar
   cheese
1 t. Worcestershire sauce

1 t. browning and seasoning
   sauce
1 t. salt
4 slices French bread, toasted

In a bowl, combine uncooked beef, cheese, sauces and salt; mix well. Spread mixture over one side of each bread slice. Place on an ungreased baking sheet. Broil for about 5 minutes, until beef is cooked through and cheese is melted. Makes 4 servings.

Treat yourself to a soda-shop specialty...a tall glass of cola
with a squirt of chocolate syrup stirred in!

Simple Tuna Sandwich

Pam Massey
Marshall, AR

Our small hometown drugstore on the square used to serve this sandwich at their old-fashioned soda fountain. Served with potato chips and a dill pickle, it's a wonderful light meal.

5-oz. can tuna, drained
2 eggs, hard-boiled, peeled
   and diced
1/3 c. onion, diced
2 dill pickle spears, diced

2 to 3 T. mayonnaise-style salad
   dressing
6 to 8 saltine crackers, crushed
8 slices white bread, toasted

Combine all ingredients except crackers and bread. Mix well; stir in crackers to desired consistency. Spread mixture on 4 toast slices; top with remaining slices and cut in half. Makes 4 servings.

Scottish Grilled Cheese

Lydia Reaume
Ontario, Canada

This is my Scottish mother's delicious version of a grilled cheese sandwich. My granddaughter always asks for this open-faced sandwich when she comes for a visit.

1 slice bread, toasted
brown sauce or steak sauce
   to taste

2 to 3 thin slices sharp
   Cheddar cheese
Optional: 1 tomato slice

Spread bread slice with sauce; top with cheese slices. Place on a broiler pan. Broil until cheese melts, 2 to 3 minutes. Top with a tomato slice, if desired. Makes one serving.

Candlelight makes any family meal feel special. Set lit votives on a footed cake stand for a quick & easy centerpiece.

Pumpkin Streusel Muffins ▶

Elizabeth Cisneros
Eastvale, CA

The best thing about fall...pumpkin goodies are everywhere! I like to use pumpkin as often as possible. This recipe can also be used to make loaves of pumpkin bread, which freeze beautifully.

3 c. sugar
1/2 c. applesauce
1/2 c. canola oil
4 eggs
2 c. canned pumpkin
2/3 c. water

3-1/3 c. all-purpose flour
2 t. baking soda
1-1/2 t. salt
1-1/2 t. cinnamon
1 t. nutmeg
1 c. chopped pecans

Combine sugar, applesauce, oil and eggs in a bowl. Beat with an electric mixer on low speed until blended; beat in pumpkin and water. In a separate bowl, whisk together flour, baking soda, salt and spices. Add flour mixture slowly to pumpkin mixture; beat on low speed just until moistened and smooth. Stir in nuts. Fill paper-lined muffin cups 2/3 full. Sprinkle with Streusel Topping. Bake at 350 degrees for 30 to 35 minutes, until a toothpick tests clean. Batter may also be divided between 2 greased 9"x5" loaf pans; add topping and bake for about one hour. Makes 2 dozen muffins or 2 loaves.

Streusel Topping:

1/3 c. brown sugar, packed
2 T. butter, room temperature

1/2 t. cinnamon
1/4 c. finely chopped pecans

Combine all ingredients; mix with a fork until crumbly.

Need a gift in a jiffy for a teacher, a neighbor or a friend with a new baby? Give a loaf of freshly baked quick bread wrapped in a pretty tea towel...it's sure to be appreciated.

Cranberry Cinnamon Bread

JoAnn Ragland
Bedford, VA

This recipe is the best for a satisfying sweet ending to a light meal! It will keep about a week. Reheated in the microwave, it tastes freshly baked.

1-1/2 c. whole-wheat flour
1/2 c. all-purpose flour
2/3 c. sugar
1/2 t. baking soda
1 t. salt

1 t. cinnamon
1 egg, beaten
14-oz. can whole-berry
  cranberry sauce
1 c. chopped walnuts

In a large bowl, mix flours, sugar, baking soda, salt and cinnamon. Add egg, cranberry sauce and walnuts. Stir just until moistened and a stiff batter forms. Pour batter into a greased 9"x5" loaf pan. Bake at 350 degrees for one hour, or until a toothpick inserted in the center tests clean. Cool in pan for 10 minutes. Turn out onto a wire rack; cool completely. Makes one loaf.

Old-time apple heads are fun to make with kids! Peel apples and dip in a mix of 1/2 cup lemon juice and 2 teaspoons salt to prevent browning. Scoop out eyes with the tip of a potato peeler; shape the nose, mouth and ears with a paring knife. Bake at 200 degrees for 4 to 5 hours, until dried, or air-dry for 2 weeks. Each will develop its own character as it dries.

Nana's Philadelphia Relish

Eileen Morris
Scranton, PA

This special recipe is from my Nana's very old handwritten recipe book. She served this delicious relish with baked ham. I always loved visiting Nana & Pop-Pop and smelling the wonderful smells coming from her kitchen. She was a wonderful cook.

1 head cabbage, finely chopped	1/4 c. brown sugar, packed
2 red and/or green peppers, finely chopped	1 T. celery seed
	3/4 t. mustard seed
1/4 c. vinegar	1-1/2 t. salt

In a large bowl, mix together cabbage and peppers. In a separate bowl, stir together remaining ingredients. Cover and refrigerate both bowls until serving time. To serve, pour vinegar mixture over cabbage mixture; toss to mix completely. Serves 8 to 12.

Walnut-Cranberry Relish

Ed Kielar
Perrysburg, OH

This relish makes any turkey dinner taste like Thanksgiving! It's the easiest recipe for cranberry relish I've used.

14-oz. can whole-berry cranberry sauce	11-oz. can mandarin oranges, drained
1/2 c. chopped walnuts	

Combine all ingredients in a serving bowl; stir gently. Cover and chill. Makes 6 servings.

Keep an eye open for vintage silver spoons at flea markets.
Tied onto giftable jars of salsa, jam, jelly or relish,
they make an ordinary gift extra special.

THANKSGIVING
Dinner to Remember

End-of-Summer Kielbasa Skillet

Sue Beyenhof
Luverne, MN

Like many gardeners, I always find it a challenge to use all my zucchini and summer squash. This dish turns it into a warm, comforting dish to enjoy on a crisp fall evening. I sometimes add home-canned tomatoes. If you have extra garden beans or corn to add, just increase the cooking time. I've made this many different ways, and it is always delicious. Enjoy!

2 T. olive oil
1 yellow onion, diced
2 c. zucchini, sliced 1-inch thick
2 c. yellow squash, sliced
   1-inch thick
3 c. chicken broth
8 to 10 new redskin potatoes,
   halved

2 c. cabbage, shredded
1 lb. Kielbasa sausage, sliced
   1/2-inch thick
6-oz. can tomato paste
1 t. salt
Optional: 1/2 t. celery salt
1/2 t. pepper

Heat oil in a deep skillet over medium heat. Sauté onion, zucchini and yellow squash until softened. Add chicken broth; bring to a boil. Add potatoes and cabbage; cook for 10 to 12 minutes. Stir in Kielbasa, tomato paste and seasonings. Cover and cook over low heat for an additional 15 minutes, or until vegetables are tender. Serves 8.

Host a back-to-school cookout and invite the families of your children's school friends. Grill foil packets filled with hamburgers and fresh veggies alongside foil-wrapped garlic bread. For dessert, how about an ice cream sundae bar? Easy and a great way to get reacquainted.

THANKSGIVING
Dinner to Remember

Cornbread Dinner Surprise

Brenda Hodson
Clinton, IN

*I created this yummy recipe with my young children
one autumn evening. It has become a family favorite!*

2 lbs. ground beef	salt and pepper to taste
2 T. onion, chopped	2 c. shredded Cheddar cheese
1-1/2 c. catsup	8-1/2 oz. pkg. cornbread mix
1/2 c. brown sugar, packed	1/2 c. milk
1-1/2 T. Worcestershire sauce	1 egg, beaten
1 t. chili powder	Garnish: sour cream
1/2 t. garlic salt	

In a skillet over medium heat, brown beef and onion. Drain; stir in
catsup, brown sugar, Worcestershire sauce and seasonings. Reduce heat
to low; cook for 15 minutes. Transfer beef mixture to a lightly greased
13"x9" baking pan. Cover with cheese. In a small bowl, stir together dry
cornbread mix, milk and egg. Pour batter over cheese. Bake, uncovered,
at 350 degrees for 20 minutes, or until bubbly and cornbread is golden.
Let cool 5 minutes. Cut into squares; serve with a dollop of sour cream.
Serves 6.

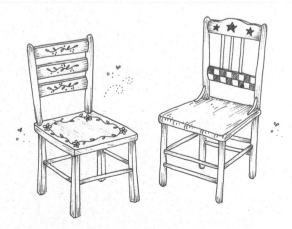

Spruce up child-size chairs with a new coat of paint and tuck
them in corners to hold a potted plant or a stack of favorite books.
They'll look so sweet at the Thanksgiving children's table too!

Tennessee Sausage & Rice

Tamela James
Grove City, OH

My husband Steve & I love to take weekend anniversary trips to Tennessee. On one trip, he picked up a cookbook with a recipe similar to a hometown restaurant's rice dish that he really liked. The first time, I followed the recipe. Then I made it several more times, tweaking to our taste with each version. This is our final version... it's yummy! We love it.

16-oz. pkg. mild ground pork
  sausage
16-oz. pkg. hot ground pork
  sausage
1.2-oz. pkg. savory herb and
  garlic soup mix

4 c. beef broth
3/4 c. celery, finely chopped
3/4 c. onion, finely chopped
3-oz. can diced green chiles
3 c. instant brown rice, uncooked
1 c. sliced mushrooms

Brown both packages of sausage in a large skillet over medium heat. Drain; add soup mix, broth, celery and onion. Cook until tender. Add chiles; bring to a boil. Stir in uncooked rice and mushrooms. Cover and cook over low heat for 5 minutes, or until tender but still partially liquid. Transfer mixture to a greased 6-quart casserole dish. Bake, uncovered, at 400 degrees for 15 to 20 minutes. Makes 8 to 10 servings.

We rely on home not to change,
and it does not,
wherefore we give thanks.

–Elizabeth Bowen

THANKSGIVING
Dinner to Remember

Chicken with Broccoli & Wild Rice
Carrie Fostor
Baltic, OH

This is a very tasty and satisfying dish...great for those autumn days when you've been busy raking leaves! Use fresh broccoli if you like, steamed until it's just crisp-tender.

6-oz. pkg. long-grain and wild
   rice mix, uncooked
2 c. cooked chicken, cubed
10-oz. pkg. frozen chopped
   broccoli, thawed and drained
4-oz. can sliced mushrooms,
   drained

1 c. shredded sharp Cheddar
   cheese
10-3/4 oz. can celery soup
1/2 c. mayonnaise
2 t. mustard
1 t. curry powder
Garnish: grated Parmesan cheese

Cook rice as package directs. In a lightly greased 2-quart casserole dish layer rice, chicken, broccoli, mushrooms and Cheddar cheese. In a separate bowl, mix together soup, mayonnaise, mustard and curry powder; spoon over top. Sprinkle with Parmesan cheese. Bake, uncovered, at 350 degrees for 45 minutes, or until hot and bubbly. Serves 6.

Set a leaf placecard at each dinner guest's place. Write each name on a leaf using a gold or silver pen...try bright green leaves in late summer, beautiful red or orange fallen leaves in autumn.

Mama's Baked Spaghetti

Norma Renaud
Ontario, Canada

Every autumn on our 50-acre farm, all of my brothers & sisters... nine of us!..would help Daddy & Mama harvest the tomatoes that Daddy grew. We ate as many from the field as we picked. After the crop was in, Mama would can up all the tomatoes for her famous baked spaghetti. I never knew spaghetti sauce came in a can until I was 12 years old! At that age, to me it was just another harvest, but now every harvest season I have the warmest memories from my childhood of tomato season and baked spaghetti.

32-oz. pkg. spaghetti, uncooked
2 lbs. ground beef
6 c. home-canned tomatoes,
   or 2 28-oz. cans whole
   tomatoes

1 t. dried oregano
2 bay leaves
salt and pepper to taste

Cook spaghetti according to package directions; drain. Meanwhile, in a large skillet over medium heat, cook beef until browned; drain. Combine spaghetti, beef, tomatoes with juice and seasonings in a lightly greased large roasting pan. Cover and bake at 325 degrees for 50 minutes to one hour, until hot and bubbly. Discard bay leaves before serving. Makes about 10 servings.

Over dinner, ask your kids to tell you about books they're reading at school and return the favor by sharing books you loved as a child....perhaps stories of small-town life like *Anne of Green Gables, Tom Sawyer* or *Little House on the Prairie.* You may find you have some favorites in common!

Bierock Casserole

Rhonda Darbro
Shell Knob, MO

This is a quick & easy alternative to making individual bierock meat pies. The recipe can easily be divided between two 8"x8" pans...one to serve now and one to freeze for later, or to share with a neighbor!

2 lbs. lean ground beef
1 onion, chopped
1/2 head cabbage, shredded
salt and pepper to taste

2 8-oz. tubes refrigerated
   crescent rolls
2 c. shredded Cheddar cheese

In a skillet over medium heat, brown beef and onion; do not drain. Add cabbage; reduce heat to low and simmer for 20 minutes. Season to taste with salt and pepper. Spray a 13"x9" baking pan with non-stick vegetable spray. Press one tube of crescent rolls into the bottom of pan, sealing perforations. Spread beef mixture over rolls; sprinkle cheese over beef mixture. Top with remaining tube of crescent rolls, sealing perforations. Bake, uncovered, at 350 degrees for 30 minutes. Cut into squares to serve. Makes 6 to 8 servings.

The weekend before Thanksgiving, invite a friend or two over to make ahead a few harvest dishes for the big day. You can even trade specialties, such as her nut bread for your special spiced apples. While you're chatting and laughing together, you'll be done in no time!

Parmesan Pork Chops

LaShelle Brown
Mulvane, KS

This recipe came from a B & B in our hometown. Boneless chicken breasts may also be used. So easy and delicious!

1 c. Italian-flavored dry bread
   crumbs
1/2 c. grated Parmesan cheese
1/2 t. paprika
1/4 t. garlic powder
1/2 t. salt

1/2 t. pepper
6 boneless pork chops,
   1-inch thick
1/4 c. olive oil
1/4 c. margarine, melted
seasoned salt to taste

In a shallow bowl, mix together bread crumbs, cheese, paprika, garlic powder, salt and pepper. Add oil to a separate shallow bowl. Dip pork chops into olive oil, then in bread crumb mixture to coat. Place pork chops on a parchment paper-lined rimmed baking sheet. Drizzle with margarine; sprinkle with seasoned salt. Bake, uncovered, at 350 degrees for one hour, or until pork chops are tender. Makes 6 servings.

Tuck Indian corn, bumpy gourds, colorful autumn leaves and
bright sunflowers into a Thanksgiving cornucopia for
a festive addition to the mantel.

Ginger & Green Onion Chicken

Laura Wilson
Oakley, CA

This dish is scrumptious, fast and easy to prepare.

1/2 c. all-purpose flour
1 t. salt
1/4 t. pepper
1/2 c. oil
5 boneless skinless chicken
    breasts, or 2 lbs. chicken
    tenderloins
1/4 c. green onions, finely sliced

1/4 c. fresh ginger, peeled and
    finely minced
2 t. cornstarch
1/2 c. hot water
1/4 c. soy sauce
2 T. sugar
1 c. chicken broth
cooked rice

Combine flour, salt and pepper in a paper bag. Add chicken to bag; toss to coat. Heat oil in a large skillet over medium heat. Add chicken; cook until golden on both sides. Remove chicken to a platter, reserving drippings; keep warm. Add onions and ginger to skillet; sauté until onions are tender. In a small bowl, combine cornstarch with hot water; blend with a fork. Add soy sauce and sugar to cornstarch mixture. Add cornstarch mixture to skillet, scraping up any browned bits in the bottom of skillet. Stir in chicken broth. Return chicken to skillet; cover and simmer for 10 to 15 minutes, until chicken juices run clear when pierced and sauce in skillet thickens. Remove chicken to a serving platter; top with sauce from skillet. Serve with cooked rice. Makes 5 servings.

Throw a pumpkin painting party! Provide washable paints, brushes and plenty of pumpkins...invite kids to bring their imagination and an old shirt to wear as a smock. Parents are sure to join in too!

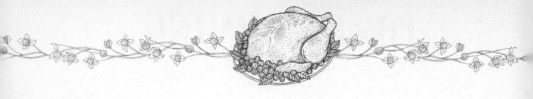

Haluski

Jessica Kraus
Delaware, OH

If you are a Polish girl who grew up in Pennsylvania, like me, then you know all about Haluski! It's a hearty stick-to-your ribs dish of sausage, noodles and cabbage....just right for a busy fall day. My whole family enjoys this dish.

1 lb. Kielbasa sausage, sliced
2 T. butter
1 head cabbage, sliced
1 onion, diced
1 apple, peeled, cored and diced
2 T. garlic, minced

1 T. cider vinegar
1 t. brown sugar, packed
salt and pepper to taste
8-oz. pkg. kluski noodles, uncooked

Heat a stockpot or Dutch oven over medium heat. Add Kielbasa and cook until golden, about 5 minutes. Remove Kielbasa to a bowl; set aside. Add butter to drippings in pan; scrape up all the brown bits in the bottom of pan. Add remaining ingredients except noodles. Reduce heat to low. Stir well; cover and cook for 30 minutes. Return Kielbasa to pan; cook an additional 15 minutes, or just until cabbage is tender. Meanwhile, cook noodles according to package directions; drain and add to cabbage mixture. Cover and let stand for 10 to 15 minutes, to allow noodles to absorb flavor. Makes 8 servings.

Have an adventure potluck...a terrific way to get together with friends old and new. Ask each guest to bring a favorite dish from their hometown...whether that's somewhere across the USA or even around the world. Remember to ask everyone to bring recipe cards to share!

Bacon & Cheddar Peroghies

Arlene Gerein
Alberta, Canada

I learned this recipe from a friend a long time ago and instantly fell in love with its flavor and simplicity. You may have some of the mashed potato filling left over...it makes great potato pancakes.

1 lb. bacon
1/4 c. onion, chopped
10 redskin potatoes
1-1/4 c. shredded sharp
   Cheddar cheese
salt and pepper to taste

16-oz. container sour cream
2 c. all-purpose flour
Garnish: sour cream, chopped
   fresh chives, French fried
   onions, crumbled bacon

In a skillet over medium heat, cook bacon until crisp. Crumble bacon and set aside; reserve drippings in skillet. Add onion to drippings; cook until soft. Meanwhile, in a separate saucepan, cover potatoes with water. Cook until tender; drain, mash and let cool. When potatoes have cooled, add bacon, onion, cheese, salt and pepper; mix well. In a large bowl, mix sour cream and flour until a sticky dough forms. On a floured surface, roll out dough 1/4-inch thick. Cut out circles of dough with a glass tumbler or empty soup can. Add more flour to surface as needed, but dough should remain sticky. Add one teaspoonful potato mixture to each circle of dough; fold dough over and pinch sides together. Place on ungreased baking sheets; cover and freeze. Transfer to plastic freezer bags, one dozen to a bag. To serve, bring a large pot of water to a boil over high heat. Add desired amount of peroghies and cook until they float to the surface, 5 to 7 minutes. Drain; serve with desired toppings. Makes 5 to 6 dozen.

Every sofa should have an inviting throw folded over the back for snuggling! Why not pull out that afghan that Great-Aunt Sophie crocheted years ago, or a treasured baby quilt that's been outgrown, for warm and cozy memories.

Chicken & Sausage Gumbo

Becky Butler
Keller, TX

Growing up in South Louisiana, the first cold snap of autumn meant it was time to make gumbo! I can remember my mother calling my grandmother or aunt to tell them she was making roux, the first step for gumbo. Invariably, both of them were making gumbo as well! Now, as an adult with my own family, I still get those silly phone calls myself!

1/2 c. all-purpose flour
1/2 c. oil
3-1/2 lbs. chicken
2 c. onion, chopped
2 c. celery, chopped
1/4 red pepper, chopped
5 to 6 cloves garlic, sliced
1 lb. smoked pork sausage or
   andouille, sliced
14-oz. can petite diced tomatoes
8 c. chicken broth
1-1/2 to 2 T. Cajun seasoning
2 bay leaves
salt and pepper to taste
1 c. fresh flat-leaf parsley,
   chopped
cooked rice

Add flour and oil to a large Dutch oven over medium heat. Stirring constantly with a flat-bottomed spoon, cook slowly until flour darkens to a dark brown milk chocolate color. Do not burn. Turn heat to medium-high. Working in batches, add chicken pieces, skin-side down. Cook until chicken is well browned but not cooked through. Remove chicken to a plate. Add sausage and cook, stirring occasionally, about 5 minutes. Remove sausage to plate. Add onion, celery and pepper to drippings; stir well to coat. Cook 3 to 5 minutes, until wilted. Add garlic; cook for 2 to 3 minutes. Return chicken and sausage to pot; add tomatoes with juice, broth, bay leaves, seasoning, salt and pepper. Bring to a simmer over high heat; reduce heat to low. Cover and simmer for one hour, stirring occasionally. Uncover and stir; simmer another 15 minutes. At serving time, stir in parsley. To serve, fill individual bowls with rice. Top each bowl with a piece of chicken, several sausage slices and some of the liquid. Serves 12.

Greet guests with a harvest welcome. Line a wheelbarrow
with straw and fill with a colorful assortment of
pumpkins and Indian corn.

Pepper Chicken & Rotini

Charlotte Smith
Tyrone, PA

A quick & very tasty one-dish dinner for a cool evening. I've also made this with sweet Italian sausage links. Just cut the sausage in one-inch slices and follow the instructions.

1 lb. boneless skinless chicken
   breasts, cubed
1 to 2 T. oil
1 green pepper, cut into strips
1 onion, sliced

1-1/2 c. water
2 c. rotini or ziti pasta, uncooked
26-oz. jar spaghetti sauce
1 c. shredded mozzarella cheese

In a large skillet over medium-high heat, cook chicken in oil for 5 minutes. Add green pepper and onion; cook another 5 minutes, stirring occasionally. Add water; bring to a boil. Add uncooked pasta. Stir until pasta is completely covered with water. Reduce heat to low. Cover and simmer for 15 minutes, or until pasta is tender. Stir in sauce; sprinkle with cheese. Cover and cook for 5 minutes, or until cheese is melted. Makes 4 to 6 servings.

Set out a variety of board games and jigsaw puzzles when family & friends are visiting. Pull out your childhood favorites... sure to spark memories and laughter!

Swiss & Halibut Bake

Cheri Maxwell
Gulf Breeze, FL

A speedy yet elegant supper to share with friends.

2 lbs. halibut fillets, thawed
salt and pepper to taste
1 T. lemon juice
3/4 c. white wine or chicken
　broth
1/4 lb. sliced mushrooms

1/4 c. butter
3 T. all-purpose flour
1 c. half-and-half
1/2 t. salt
1 c. shredded Swiss cheese

Arrange fish in a lightly greased 13"x9" baking pan; season with salt and pepper. Drizzle with lemon juice and wine or broth. Cover and bake at 400 degrees for 12 to 15 minutes, until fish flakes easily with a fork. Remove from oven; drain, reserving liquid. Meanwhile, in a skillet over medium heat, sauté mushrooms in butter; stir in flour. Add half-and-half and reserved liquid to skillet; cook and stir until thickened and smooth. Add salt and cheese; stir until cheese melts. Spoon sauce over fish. Bake, uncovered, for about 10 minutes. Serves 4 to 6.

Lemon-Parsley Butter

Samantha Starks
Madison, WI

A pat of this savory butter adds flavor to chicken, fish and steamed veggies. It's handy to keep tucked in the freezer...no need to thaw, just slice thinly and add to hot foods.

1/2 c. butter, softened
1 T. lemon zest
1/2 t. dried oregano

1/4 t. dried parsley
1/4 t garlic salt
1/8 t. pepper

Combine all ingredients in a bowl; blend well. Form into a log and seal in plastic wrap, or spoon into a small covered container. Chill for 4 hours to allow flavors to blend. Makes 1/2 cup.

Fancy Faux Crab

Michelle Marberry
Valley, AL

Quick, easy and impressive...perfect for company!

2 cloves garlic, minced
2 T. butter
2 lbs. imitation crabmeat, flaked
1/2 c. chicken broth

8-oz. pkg. shredded Monterey
   Jack cheese
1 T. dried parsley
cooked angel hair pasta or rice

In a skillet over medium-high heat, sauté garlic in butter for one minute. Add crabmeat; cook for 4 minutes. With a slotted spoon, transfer crab to a lightly greased 11"x7" baking pan; set aside and keep warm. Add broth to skillet over medium heat; bring to a boil. Cook and stir for 5 minutes, or until broth is slightly reduced. Drizzle over crabmeat; top with cheese and parsley. Bake, uncovered, at 350 degrees for 10 minutes, or until cheese is melted. Serve over cooked pasta or rice. Serves 6.

"Adopt" an older neighbor as a grandparent. Include him or her in the children's ball games and family outings...bake cookies together and share stories over dinner. Your family can help out by weeding flower beds, raking leaves and running errands...it's sure to be rewarding for everybody!

Coco's Herbed Roast Turkey

Colleen Ludgate
Ontario, Canada

I serve this turkey for every holiday, and it's always perfectly juicy and tender...gravy is optional! Basting is the secret, so set your timer. I find it's best when the turkey is roasted unstuffed.

2 carrots, peeled and coarsely
   chopped
2 stalks celery, coarsely chopped
1 onion, coarsely chopped
2 to 4 14-1/2 oz. cans chicken
   broth, divided
12 to 14-lb. turkey, thawed
   if frozen
2 lemons, halved
6 T. butter, divided

1 T. dried parsley
1 T. dried sage
1 T. dried paprika
1 T. dried thyme
1 T. garlic powder
1 T. onion powder
1/2 t. salt
1/2 t. pepper
2 yds. cotton cheesecloth

Place vegetables in a roasting pan; pour in 2 cans chicken broth. Place turkey in pan; place lemons inside turkey. Slice 2 tablespoons butter; loosen skin over breast and place butter under skin. Melt remaining butter; mix with seasonings. Brush butter mixture over turkey. Unfold cheesecloth into a strip 4 layers thick and wide enough to cover turkey. Dip cheesecloth into broth in pan; drape over turkey, covering completely. Insert a meat thermometer in thickest part of thigh. Bake, uncovered, at 325 degrees, for 3 to 3-3/4 hours. Use a turkey baster to baste with pan juices every 30 minutes. Add remaining broth as needed if pan begins to get dry. One hour before turkey is done, use baster to thoroughly soak cheesecloth with pan juices. Use tongs to carefully remove cheesecloth. Continue baking, basting once again at final 30 minutes, until skin is golden and crisp and thermometer reads 165 to 170 degrees. Remove turkey to a serving platter; let stand for 20 minutes before carving. Serves 8 to 10.

Garnish the turkey platter with tiny pickled crabapples
and sprigs of fresh sage...so pretty!

THANKSGIVING
Dinner to Remember

Sourdough Mushroom Stuffing

Leah Dodson
Covington, KY

Four years ago, my husband and I bought our first home. We wanted to host a Thanksgiving dinner but since both of our families have their own traditions, we decided to start our own. We call it "Friendsgiving," and we invite all of our friends over on the Saturday after Thanksgiving. After a hearty meal, we play board games until it's time for dessert. I found this flavorful recipe a few years ago...hope you enjoy it as much as we do!

3 T. butter, divided
1 lb. assorted wild or white
   mushrooms, sliced
3 c. celery, chopped
2 c. onion, finely chopped
1-lb. loaf sourdough bread,
   cubed
1-1/2 c. low-sodium chicken
   broth
1/2 c. fresh flat-leaf parsley,
   chopped
1 T. fresh thyme, chopped
1 T. fresh sage, chopped
1 t. fresh rosemary, chopped
2 t. salt
1 t. pepper

Coat a 3-quart casserole dish with one tablespoon butter; set aside. Melt remaining butter in a large saucepan over medium-high heat. Add mushrooms and sauté for 10 minutes. Add celery and onion; sauté for 10 minutes. Remove from heat. Add remaining ingredients and toss to combine. Spoon mixture into casserole dish; cover with aluminum foil. Bake at 350 degrees for 45 minutes; remove foil and bake for an additional 20 minutes, until golden. Makes 9 to 12 servings.

Serve a savory side dish baked in a pumpkin. Hollow out a pumpkin, spoon in the filling and replace the top. Set pumpkin on a rimmed baking sheet. Bake at 350 degrees for about one to 1-1/2 hours, until filling is heated through and pumpkin is tender.

Spiced Holiday Ham

Lora Christensen
Snowflake, AZ

My husband & I were newlyweds when my mother asked us to bring a ham for Thanksgiving. I panicked, thinking of purchasing sliced deli ham. We asked my mother-in-law, who's a wonderful cook, for help. She gave me this recipe that's very easy to remember and put together. You really can't mess it up! Later, all three of my sisters called to ask me for the recipe so they could serve this ham to their families at Christmas.

10 to 12-lb. fully cooked
    bone-in ham
3 T. cinnamon
2 T. ground cloves
2 t. nutmeg
16-oz. pkg. brown sugar
30-oz. can crushed pineapple

Place ham in an ungreased roasting pan. Mix spices in a small bowl; rub over ham. In a separate bowl, mix brown sugar and pineapple with juices; spoon over ham. Insert a meat thermometer in center of ham without touching bone. Cover and bake at 325 degrees for 2-1/4 to 2-3/4 hours, until thermometer reads 140 degrees. Remove ham to a serving platter; let stand for 20 minutes before slicing. Makes about 20 servings.

Share the Thanksgiving bounty...call a local college and
invite an out-of-town student to dinner who isn't
going home over the long weekend.

Noodles Romanoff

Sheila Plock
Boalsburg, PA

An easy and elegant side for baked ham or roast pork.

8-oz. pkg. narrow egg noodles,
   uncooked
2 t. margarine
2 c. sour cream
1 t. fresh chives, snipped

1 to 2 cloves garlic, pressed
1 t. salt
1/8 t. pepper
1/2 c. grated Parmesan cheese,
   divided

Cook noodles according to package directions; drain. Transfer hot noodles to a serving bowl; add margarine and toss to coat. In a separate bowl, combine remaining ingredients, reserving 1/4 cup cheese. Add sour cream mixture to hot noodles; toss to mix and top with reserved cheese. Serves 6 to 8.

Honey-Mustard Slaw

Melissa Currie
Phoenix, AZ

This zesty slaw is fantastic with any kind of barbecue...
perfect for autumn tailgating!

1/2 c. mayonnaise
1/2 c. sour cream
2 T. honey
1 to 2 T. Dijon mustard
5 c. shredded coleslaw mix

Optional: 1/4 c. sliced green
   onions
Optional: 1 jicama, peeled and
   shredded
1/2 to 1 c. chopped pecans

In a bowl, mix mayonnaise, sour cream, honey and mustard. Cover and refrigerate up to one day in advance. Shortly before serving time, combine coleslaw mix and optional ingredients, if using, in a serving bowl. Add mayonnaise mixture; toss to coat. Add pecans to taste; mix again and serve immediately. Serves 6.

Cloth napkins are so much nicer than paper ones! Make napkin rings of grapevine and hot glue a different button to each.

Johnny Bull Turkey & Onions

Paulette Lowe
Milroy, PA

*This recipe was handed down through my husband's mother's family.
I remember thinking "yuck" when they said we were having this for
Thanksgiving...but now it isn't Thanksgiving without Johnny Bull!*

3 lbs. yellow onions, quartered
1 loaf sliced white bread
1/4 to 1/2 c. butter, softened
2 t. poultry seasoning

2 t. salt
12 to 14-lb. turkey, thawed
    if frozen
mashed potatoes

In a large saucepan, cover onions with water. Cook over medium heat
until tender; drain. Toast bread and spread with butter; tear each slice
into 6 pieces. Add bread and seasonings to onions; mix well. Place
turkey in a roasting pan; spoon onion mixture around turkey. Insert a
meat thermometer in thickest part of thigh. Bake, uncovered, at
325 degrees, for 3 to 3-3/4 hours, until thermometer reads 165 degrees.
Cover with aluminum foil if turkey is browning too quickly. Remove
turkey to a platter and let stand for 20 minutes; slice. Spoon onion
mixture into a serving bowl; serve over mashed potatoes.
Serves 8 to 10.

Thanksgiving Poultry Seasoning

Sharon Demers
Dolores, CO

*This seasoning makes roast turkey and chicken, dressing
and pot pies taste wonderful!*

1 T. dried rosemary
1 T. dried oregano
1 T. dried marjoram
1 T. dried thyme

1 T. ground ginger
1 t. dried sage
1 t. pepper

Mix all ingredients in a mini food processor. Process until well mixed.
Store in an airtight container. Makes 1/2 cup.

Make-Ahead Turkey Gravy

Lisa Songster
Martinez, CA

This recipe can be made up to a month ahead of time. Avoid the hassle of making gravy just before everyone sits down to dinner! Freshly ground pepper is the best.

3 to 4 lbs. turkey wings and/or
  drumsticks
2 onions, coarsely chopped
1 c. water
8 c. chicken broth, divided

1 carrot, coarsely chopped
1/2 t. dried thyme
3/4 c. all-purpose flour
2 T. butter
1/2 t. pepper

Place turkey pieces in an ungreased 13"x9" baking pan. Scatter onions over turkey. Bake, uncovered, at 400 degrees for about 1-1/4 hours, until golden. Remove turkey and onions to a large stockpot; set aside. Pour water into roasting pan; stir to loosen browned bits in bottom. Add water to stockpot along with 6 cups broth, carrot and thyme. Bring to a boil over medium heat. Reduce heat to low and simmer, uncovered, for 1-1/2 hours. Remove turkey from stockpot; reserve for another use. Strain broth mixture into a separate large saucepan; cover and refrigerate for several hours to overnight. Skim fat. Bring broth mixture to a gentle boil. Whisk flour into remaining broth, until smooth; whisk into boiling broth mixture. Boil and stir for 5 minutes, until thickened. Stir in butter and pepper. Pour gravy into a freezer-safe container; freeze for up to one month. To serve, thaw and reheat. Drippings from a freshly roasted turkey may be added at serving time, if desired. Makes about 8 cups.

Going home for Thanksgiving? Take a little time to show your children all the places you loved as a child...the school play yard, the public library, the corner candy store. You'll be making brand new memories!

Buttercup Squash & Apple Bake

Sara Tatham
Plymouth, NH

Many years ago when we were newly married, my husband wanted to spend an autumn day helping his dad and brothers harvest firewood. I wanted to go along, but I needed to make a harvest dish to take to a church potluck that night. My husband's grandfather had told me I could cook in his kitchen, so I brought along my ingredients. When Grampa saw what I planned to make, he insisted on peeling the apples for me with his hand-cranked apple peeler. What a fun memory we made in his little kitchen that day! The dish turned out delicious, too. Now I have been making this recipe for over 30 years. It's nice at Thanksgiving or with any autumn meal.

3-lb. buttercup or butternut
   squash, halved, seeds
   removed, peeled and sliced
   1/2-inch thick
3 apples, cored and sliced
   1/2-inch thick

6 T. margarine, melted
2/3 c. brown sugar, packed
1-1/2 T. all-purpose flour
1-1/4 t. salt

Arrange squash slices in a lightly greased 13"x9" baking pan. Arrange apple slices on top of squash. Mix remaining ingredients; sprinkle over top. Cover tightly with aluminum foil. Bake at 350 degrees for about one hour, or until squash is tender. Serves 6 to 8.

Write harvest quotes on strips of paper and fasten around drinking glasses with double-sided tape. When Thanksgiving guests are seated, invite them to read the quotes aloud.

Maple Whipped Sweet Potatoes

Gary-Lee Gordon
Olathe, KS

I used to wait all year for fall, when my family came together and we would enjoy this dish as one of the star sides at the holiday table. It's simple yet flavorful, so now we enjoy it year 'round.

4 sweet potatoes, peeled, cubed
    and cooked
1 t. orange zest, or more to taste

2 T. butter, melted
3 T. maple syrup

In a large bowl, mash sweet potatoes with an electric mixer on medium-low speed. Beat in orange zest. Transfer mixture into a greased 2-quart casserole dish. In a small bowl, mix butter and syrup; drizzle over sweet potato mixture. Bake, uncovered, at 350 degrees for about 25 minutes, until heated through. Serves 6.

Keep a basket of picnic supplies in your car for picnics at a moment's notice. With a quilt or tablecloth, paper napkins, plates and cups you'll always be ready. Just pick up some sandwich fixin's and drinks and you're ready to go!

Smashed Potatoes

Lisa Ann Panzino DiNunzio
Vineland, NJ

A super yummy side that my family can't seem to get enough of!

12 new potatoes
4 to 6 T. extra virgin olive oil

garlic powder, dried parsley,
salt and pepper to taste

Cover potatoes with salted water in a saucepan. Bring to a boil over medium-high heat. Cook until fork-tender, 10 to 15 minutes; drain. Generously drizzle olive oil on a rimmed baking sheet. Arrange potatoes on baking sheet, one to 2 inches apart. With a potato masher, gently press down each potato until slightly flattened. Turn baking sheet 90 degrees and flatten potatoes again. Drizzle with more oil; sprinkle with seasonings. Broil just until crisp and golden on both sides. Serves 4 to 6.

Tuck a fall floral arrangement of yellow spider mums and orange gerbera daisies into a vintage soup tureen...a whimsical table decoration for a casual supper. Florist foam will hold everything in place.

Brussels Sprouts & Shallots

Lori Rosenberg
University Heights, OH

*This quick & easy recipe will make any fussy vegetable eater
a member of the Brussels sprouts fan club!*

2 T. olive oil
1 c. shallots, thinly sliced
2 cloves garlic, minced
1 t. sugar

3/4 lb. Brussels sprouts, trimmed
  and sliced
1/4 t. salt
1/8 t. pepper

Heat a large heavy skillet over medium-high heat. Add oil; swirl to coat skillet. Add shallots; sauté for 3 minutes, or until almost tender, stirring occasionally. Add garlic; cook and stir for 30 seconds. Add sugar and Brussels sprouts; sauté for 5 minutes, or until golden and crisp-tender, stirring occasionally. Sprinkle with salt and pepper; toss. Serves 4.

Lay a blank card on each dinner plate and invite guests of
all ages to write down what they are most thankful for this year.
Afterwards, bind the cards together with a ribbon to
create a sweet gratitude book.

Kickin' Carrot Casserole

Carol Hickman
Kingsport, TN

*Last Thanksgiving morning, I woke up with my back in severe pain.
Thankfully, my daughter Sharlyn, who usually doesn't like to cook,
pitched in and did all the cooking for me...with me giving her how-to
tips from the couch, of course! We came up with this version of carrot
casserole that day, and it was a big hit with all the family. I have a
sweet memory of this Thanksgiving when I recall how my precious
daughter so willingly did all the cooking when I was unable to.*

3 16-oz. cans sliced carrots,
   drained
3 eggs, lightly beaten
3/4 c. sugar
1/4 c. brown sugar, packed
1/2 c. butter, softened
3 T. all-purpose flour

1 t. baking powder
1 t. cinnamon
1/2 to 1 t. ground ginger
8 to 10 gingersnaps, finely
   crushed
Optional: 1/2 c. finely chopped
   pecans or walnuts

In a large bowl, mash carrots well with a potato masher. Add eggs and
sugars; stir to combine. Add butter, flour, baking powder and spices.
With an electric mixer on medium speed, beat mixture until smooth.
Spread mixture in a 2-quart casserole dish that has been lightly sprayed
with butter-flavored non-stick vegetable spray. Sprinkle with gingersnap
crumbs and nuts, if desired. Bake, uncovered, at 400 degrees for
15 minutes. Reduce heat to 350 degrees; bake an additional 40 to
45 minutes. Makes 8 to 10 servings.

Start a holiday journal...decorate
a blank book, then use it to note
each year's special moments,
meals enjoyed, guests welcomed
and gifts given. You'll love
looking back on these
happy memories!

Nonnie's Baked Zucchini

Kathleen Walker
Mountain Center, CA

I always looked forward to weekends with my great-grandparents. Great-Grandmother Nonnie was a baker, a quilter and a wonderful cook. I loved all the aromas that wafted from her busy kitchen, including this delicious baked zucchini...mmm!

8 zucchini, halved lengthwise	salt and pepper to taste
1/2 onion, chopped	1/2 c. shredded Cheddar cheese
1 to 2 t. oil	1 c. toasted bread crumbs
2 eggs, beaten	paprika to taste
1 c. cottage cheese	Garnish: chopped fresh parsley
1/2 c. buttermilk	

Place zucchini in a lightly greased 13"x9" glass baking pan, cut-side up. Cover and bake at 350 degrees until partially tender, about 15 to 20 minutes; remove from oven. Meanwhile, in a small skillet, sauté onion in oil; drain. Beat together eggs, cottage cheese, buttermilk, salt and pepper; stir in onion mixture. Spoon mixture over zucchini. Sprinkle with shredded cheese and bread crumbs; dust with paprika. Bake for an additional 15 minutes. Garnish with parsley. Serves 8 to 10.

After the last Thanksgiving dish is passed, get all the kids together and have the older relatives teach them how to play some nostalgic games like hopscotch, horseshoes and jump-rope...sure to shake off that ate-too-much feeling and get a lot of laughs!

Brenda's Famous Green Chile Potatoes

Brenda Schlosser
Brighton, CO

I created this potato recipe 15 years ago when I worked for the phone company in Sacramento. I took it often to potlucks...I could hardly get in the door before I was attacked by people wanting some at 8 a.m.! You don't even have to peel the potatoes.

4 to 5 baking potatoes, thinly
    sliced and divided
garlic powder, salt and pepper
    to taste
12-oz. container sour cream,
    divided
1 to 1-1/2 c. canned roasted
    green chiles

6 green onions, chopped
1 lb. bacon, crisply cooked and
    crumbled
2 c. shredded Cheddar cheese
1 T. Worcestershire sauce
1/4 c. butter, sliced

Arrange half of potato slices, slightly overlapping, in a greased 13"x9" baking pan. Sprinkle with seasonings; spread half of sour cream over potatoes. Layer with chiles, remaining sour cream, onions, bacon, cheese, remaining potatoes, additional seasonings and Worcestershire sauce. Dot with butter. Cover with aluminum foil. Bake at 375 degrees for 60 to 75 minutes, until potatoes are tender. Serves 8 to 10.

Head to the pumpkin patch, ride a hay wagon, run through a corn maze...fall is full of wonderful activities for the young and young-at-heart!

Indiana Corn Pudding

Claire Bertram
Lexington, KY

Gramma's old-fashioned corn pudding was
a "must" every Thanksgiving!

4 green onions, finely chopped
2 T. butter
1 T. all-purpose flour
3 eggs, lightly beaten
2 c. milk

1 t. salt
1/2 t. pepper
2 10-oz. pkgs. frozen corn,
   thawed, or 3 c. fresh corn

In a small skillet over low heat, sauté onions in butter until wilted, 7 to 10 minutes. Stir in flour and blend well; remove from heat. In a large bowl, whisk together eggs, milk, salt and pepper. Add onion mixture and corn to egg mixture; mix well. Pour into a greased shallow 2-quart casserole dish. Set dish in a slightly larger baking pan. Pour hot water into large pan, halfway up the sides of the casserole dish. Bake, uncovered, at 325 degrees for one hour, or until set and edges are lightly golden. Serves 6.

Spend a sunny autumn day at a nearby fair...just about every county has one! You'll discover terrific things...beautiful handmade quilts, displays of prize-winning produce, rows of colorful canned goods and some of the best food ever.

Holiday Stuffing Balls

Laura Flores
Middletown, CT

When I was young, my whole family would pile into our cherry-red Ford LTD station wagon and head to the small college town where our father went to school. When we got there, our parents would buy us fresh doughnuts...a huge treat for us! Then we watched the homecoming parade with our cousins. We loved listening to the bands and seeing the decorated floats, the beauty queens and baton twirlers. We tried to catch the candy they flung to us. Afterwards, we would gather at our aunt & uncle's house for a delicious meal, and we children would play for hours. These stuffing balls were one of my favorites. I hope you enjoy this recipe as much as I do!

24-oz. loaf sliced bread, cubed
   and dried, or 14-oz. pkg.
   stuffing cubes
1/2 c. butter
2 onions, finely chopped
4 stalks celery, finely chopped
3 eggs, beaten

1 t. dried sage
1 t. salt
1/2 t. pepper
10-3/4 oz. can cream of chicken
   soup, divided
1-1/4 c. turkey or chicken broth

Place bread or stuffing cubes in a large bowl; set aside. Melt butter in a large skillet over medium heat. Sauté onions and celery until softened and golden. Pour onion mixture over bread; add eggs, seasonings and half of soup. Mix well and form into 18 balls, using about 1/3 cup mixture for each ball. Arrange in a greased 13"x9" baking pan. Combine remaining soup with broth in a small saucepan and heat, stirring until smooth. Spoon one tablespoon of soup mixture over each stuffing ball. Cover pan with aluminum foil. Bake at 350 degrees for 30 minutes. Remove foil; spoon remaining soup mixture over balls. Bake, uncovered, for an additional 10 minutes. Makes 18 servings.

A sweet keepsake for Thanksgiving dinner. Copy one of
Grandma's tried & true recipes onto a festive card, then punch
a hole in the corner and tie the card to a rolled napkin
with a length of ribbon.

THANKSGIVING
Dinner to Remember

Gail's Green Bean Bake

Gail Ebey
Canal Fulton, OH

Green bean casserole has always been a staple at family holiday meals. I wanted something other than the usual one made with canned soup...this recipe is deliciously different!

12-oz. pkg. sliced mushrooms
2 to 3 T. butter
1 c. chicken broth
2 t. all-purpose flour
3/4 c. evaporated milk

1/4 c. half-and-half
2 14-1/2 oz. cans no-salt-added
    green beans, drained
Optional: 2.8-oz. can French-
    fried onions

In a skillet over medium heat, sauté mushrooms in butter until tender; cool briefly. Add mushrooms to a food processor; process until chopped. In a separate saucepan, combine mushrooms and chicken broth. Add flour; whisk well. Stir in milk and half-and-half; simmer over low heat until thickened. Stir in beans; transfer to an ungreased 2-quart casserole dish. Bake, uncovered, at 350 degrees for 20 minutes, until hot and bubbly. Top with onions, if desired. Serves 8 to 10.

What's your hurry? Take the road less traveled on your next family trip...you'll see farmstands, charming small towns and scenic views that you might miss otherwise.

Marinated Green Beans

Vickie

A zesty blend that we enjoy year 'round.

4 c. green beans, trimmed
1 clove garlic, halved
1 onion, thinly sliced
2 T. sugar
1 t. paprika
1/4 t. salt

1 t. dried oregano
2 t. fresh parsley, chopped
1/2 t. mustard
5 T. vinegar
1/4 c. olive oil

Steam green beans until crisp-tender; drain. Rub cut sides of garlic over a wooden salad bowl. Combine beans and onion in bowl; set aside. In a small bowl, combine remaining ingredients except oil. Add oil, one tablespoon at a time, whisking well. Drizzle over bean mixture; toss lightly. Cover and refrigerate one hour to overnight. Serve warm or chilled. Serves 6 to 8.

Scandinavian Pickled Beets

Barb Rudyk
Alberta, Canada

These tangy treats add gorgeous color to any table. Great for holiday meals as well as summer barbecues. So simple to make!

15-oz. can sliced beets, drained
1/2 c. vinegar
1/2 c. water

1/2 c. sugar
salt and pepper to taste

Arrange beets in a glass or ceramic bowl; set aside. Combine remaining ingredients in a saucepan; bring to a boil. Cook and stir until sugar dissolves. Pour hot mixture over beets. Cover and refrigerate for 12 hours. Drain; serve chilled. Makes 6 servings.

A jar of homemade pickles or relish makes a welcome gift. If it's fresh, not preserved, be sure to spoon in enough liquid to cover the veggies. Tie on a tag that says "Keep refrigerated."

GAME DAY
Get-Together

Yummy Meatball Sliders

JoAnn

We love these flavorful bite-size sandwiches...and they're so easy to handle on a party buffet.

2 slices white bread, torn
1/2 c. milk
3/4 lb. ground beef
1/2 lb. ground pork
1 c. grated Parmesan cheese, divided

1 egg, beaten
3 T. fresh parsley, chopped
1 clove garlic, minced
1 t. salt
26-oz. jar pasta sauce, divided
2 doz. mini sandwich buns, split

Place bread in a large bowl; pour milk over bread and let stand for 5 minutes. Add meats, 1/2 cup Parmesan cheese, egg, parsley, garlic and salt; mix well with your hands. Cover and chill for 30 minutes. Form mixture into 2 dozen 2-inch meatballs, flattening slightly. Place meatballs in a stockpot over medium heat. Spoon one cup sauce over meatballs; bring to a simmer. Partially cover and simmer until meatballs are cooked through, about 20 to 25 minutes. Arrange bottoms of rolls on a baking sheet. Top each with one meatball, a tablespoon of remaining sauce and a teaspoon of remaining cheese. Bake, uncovered, at 400 degrees for 3 to 5 minutes, until cheese melts. Add tops of buns. Makes 2 dozen.

Arrange blazing red autumn leaves on a clear glass plate, then top with another glass plate to hold them in place...so pretty for serving an assortment of cheeses. Add a crock of hearty mustard and a basket of crackers for delicious snacking in a snap!

GAME DAY
Get-Together

Buffalo Chicken Sliders

Krista Marshall
Fort Wayne, IN

*We love buffalo wings, but they're so messy to serve at parties!
These mini sandwiches give us the same flavors with no mess. Serve
with my terrific homemade blue cheese dressing.*

2 to 3 T. butter
4 c. cooked chicken, shredded
12-oz. bottle cayenne hot pepper
  sauce

salt and pepper to taste
12 slider buns, split
Optional: crumbled blue cheese

Melt butter in a large skillet over medium heat. Add chicken; sauté for
about 5 minutes, until edges are golden and slightly crisp. Stir in desired
amount of hot sauce; season with salt and pepper. Heat until warmed
through. Spread Blue Cheese Dressing on each half of buns. Spoon
chicken mixture onto bottom halves of buns; add blue cheese, if desired,
and tops of buns. Makes one dozen.

Blue Cheese Dressing:

3/4 c. crumbled blue cheese
3/4 c. mayonnaise
6 T. sour cream

1-1/2 T. cider vinegar
1/8 t. garlic powder
1/4 t. pepper

Mix together all ingredients in a bowl; cover and chill well. Keep
refrigerated.

Everybody loves a tailgating
party...and a small-town college
rivalry can be just as much fun as
a Big Ten game. Load up a pickup
truck with tasty finger foods,
sandwiches and a big washtub
full of bottled drinks on ice.

Fresh Harvest Bruschetta

Hannah Tucker
Fallon, NV

We are blessed to have an organic farming family at our church, so when harvest time comes around, we always take home a few squash or zucchini on Sunday. I have to get creative so that the kids will eat them!

2 yellow squash or zucchini,
   halved lengthwise and
   thinly sliced
2 T. olive oil
2 tomatoes, diced
1 clove garlic, pressed
4 saltine crackers, crushed

1 t. dried oregano
1/2 t. dried basil
1/2 t. salt
1/8 t. pepper
1/2 c. shredded Cheddar cheese
1/4 c. shredded Parmesan cheese

Place squash or zucchini slices on a wire rack set in a rimmed baking sheet; brush lightly with olive oil. Adjust oven rack to second space from the top. Broil squash until lightly golden, about 5 minutes. In a bowl, mix tomatoes, garlic, crackers and seasonings. Spoon mixture evenly over squash; return to oven for 2 minutes. Sprinkle with cheeses. Broil until cheese is sizzling, about 3 minutes. Serves 8.

At holiday dinners, use a special tablecloth and ask family members, friends and special visitors to sign it with fabric markers. Sure to become a cherished tradition!

GAME DAY
Get-Together

Jane's Antipasto Squares

Jane Granger
Manteno, IL

*One stop at the deli counter and you'll have
most of the ingredients for this party-perfect treat!*

2 8-oz. tubes refrigerated
   crescent rolls
1/4 lb. sliced deli baked ham
1/4 lb. sliced provolone cheese
1/4 lb. sliced deli Genoa salami
1/4 lb. sliced Swiss cheese

1/4 lb. sliced pepperoni
12-oz. jar roasted red peppers,
   drained
3 eggs, beaten
1 T. grated Parmesan cheese
1 T. pepper

Unroll one tube of crescent rolls; do not separate rolls. Arrange rolls in
the bottom of a lightly greased 13"x9" glass baking pan. Layer meats
and cheeses in the order listed; add peppers. In a small bowl, whisk
eggs with Parmesan cheese and pepper. Pour over top, reserving a small
amount. Unroll remaining tube of crescent rolls without separating.
Place rolls on top; brush with reserved egg mixture. Cover with
aluminum foil. Bake at 350 degrees for 35 to 40 minutes. Remove foil;
bake until top is lightly golden, about 5 minutes. Cool slightly; cut into
squares. Serves 6 to 8.

Light the front walk with canning-jar luminarias on Halloween!
Paint jars with scary or funny faces on jars using acrylic paint
and nestle tealights in several inches of sand.

Sun-Dried Tomato Spread

Teanda Smith
Saint Albans, ME

This is so good! I have to make it for all of my family's parties.

1 T. garlic, minced
1 T. olive oil
1/4 c. water-packed sun-dried
   tomatoes, drained and
   chopped

1/4 c. water
8-oz. package cream cheese,
   room temperature
snack crackers

In a small skillet on medium-low heat, sauté garlic in oil until softened. Add tomatoes and stir to coat; add water and simmer until tomatoes are plumped. Drain if necessary. In a bowl, mash tomato mixture into cream cheese. Serve on crackers. Makes one cup.

Chile-Corn Hot Dip

Jennifer Tolbert
Loganville, GA

A tasty recipe to use up the last of the summer sweet corn! Other times of year, substitute 3 cups frozen corn, thawed.

6 ears fresh sweet corn
4-oz. can diced green chiles
1/2 c. mayonnaise
2 c. shredded Pepper Jack cheese

1 c. shredded Cheddar cheese
3 T. fresh cilantro, chopped
1 clove garlic, pressed
tortilla chips

Bring a large pot of water to a boil over high heat; add corn and cook for 4 to 5 minutes. Cut kernels off the cobs. In a bowl, combine corn, green chiles with juices and remaining ingredients except chips; mix well. Pour into a lightly greased 8"x8" baking pan. Bake, uncovered, at 350 degrees for 20 minutes, or until hot and bubbly. Serve with tortilla chips. Makes 12 servings.

For a quick & tasty appetizer, spread toasted baguette slices with cream cheese and top with a dollop of cranberry sauce.

Pepper Jelly Paté

*Nan Calcagno
Grosse Tete, LA*

*A terrific way to use that jar of pepper jelly
from your hometown farmers' market.*

1-1/2 c. finely shredded Cheddar
  cheese
1 c. mayonnaise
1 c. finely chopped pecans
1/4 c. green onions, chopped

salt and pepper to taste
1-1/2 c. green or yellow pepper
  jelly
crackers or corn chips

In a bowl, combine cheese, mayonnaise, pecans, onions, salt and
pepper. Blend well; spread on a serving platter. Cover with plastic wrap;
chill for 8 hours to overnight. At serving time, top with pepper jelly.
Serve with crackers or corn chips. Serves 12 to 14.

Cheddar-Pecan Spread

*Annette Ceravolo
Hoover, AL*

*This spread is such a hit at family get-togethers or entertaining
friends that I always double the recipe! It can be made
the day before...a handy make-ahead.*

3/4 c. mayonnaise
1/2 c. pecans, toasted and finely
  chopped
4 slices bacon, crisply cooked
  and finely chopped

2 T. green onions, finely chopped
8-oz. pkg. shredded Cheddar
  cheese
bread slices or crackers

In a bowl, stir together mayonnaise, pecans, bacon and onions until
well combined. Add cheese; blend well. Pack into a small serving bowl.
Cover and chill for 2 hours to overnight. Serve at room temperature with
bread or crackers. Makes 2 cups.

Smoky Salmon Tarts

Vickie

Hearty enough for a homecoming party, yet elegant enough for a ladies' luncheon! Your guests will love these savory tarts.

24 wonton wrappers
8-oz. pkg. cream cheese,
   softened
8-oz. pkg. shredded sharp
   Cheddar cheese, divided

8-oz. pkg. smoked salmon,
   flaked
6 green onions, sliced
Garnish: additional sliced green
   onions

Spray 24 mini muffin cups with non-stick vegetable spray. Gently press a wonton wrapper into each muffin cup; set aside. In a bowl, blend cream cheese and half of Cheddar cheese. Add salmon and onions; mix well. Spoon mixture into wonton cups; sprinkle with remaining Cheddar cheese. Bake at 425 degrees for 10 minutes, or until wontons are crisp and golden and cheese is melted. Garnish with additional green onions. Makes 2 dozen.

A two or three-tier pie stand is ideal for serving a variety of appetizers...just fill with goodies galore!

Pesto Pizza Squares

Meg Dickinson
Champaign, IL

This flavorful snack is a perfect appetizer during the holiday season because the colors are so festive. It's easy to make too.

11-oz. tube refrigerated pizza
  crust
1/2 c. pesto sauce
2 T. low-fat or regular
  mayonnaise

8-oz. pkg. shredded mozzarella
  cheese
1 c. cherry tomatoes, halved, or
  to taste

Roll out crust on a greased baking sheet or pizza stone; set aside. In a bowl, mix pesto, mayonnaise and cheese; spread on crust. Arrange tomatoes evenly on top. Bake at 400 degrees for 13 to 17 minutes, until crust is golden. Cut into squares, making sure each square gets a few tomato halves. Makes 8 to 12 servings.

Invite your best friends from high school to a mini reunion. Meet at your house the night of the homecoming game...hand out pom-poms in school colors and big "Class of 'XX" buttons to wear. Share snacks, beverages and memories, then cheer on your old school's football team!

Down-Home Hot Dog Chili

Cathy Matthews
Wise, VA

This recipe was passed down to me by my Aunt Edna, who worked in several restaurants in our small Virginia hometown. It makes wonderful chili dogs, chili buns and nachos with chili and cheese. It also freezes well...just spoon into freezer-safe containers.

5 lbs. ground beef
1 c. water
3 T. chili powder

3 T. paprika
2 T. salt
1 T. pepper

Place uncooked beef in a large stockpot; pour water over beef. Mix together seasonings in a small bowl; sprinkle over beef and mix well. Bring to a boil over medium heat. Reduce heat to low. Cover and simmer for 3 hours, mashing frequently with a potato masher to a chili consistency. Serve as desired. Makes 20 servings.

Arrange baby veggies in a cornucopia basket for dipping!
Cherry tomatoes, snow peas, baby corn and mini mushrooms
are all pleasing to the eye and to the tastebuds.

GAME DAY
Get-Together

Pickle-O's

Julie Pak
Henryetta, OK

Our local drive-in used to serve these deep-fried pickles, but no longer...everyone in town misses them. So, I started experimenting and came up with a recipe that is close. My family begs for them!

2 c. dill pickle slices, drained
2/3 c. all-purpose flour
1/3 c. yellow cornmeal

1 c. buttermilk
2 c. oil for deep frying
Garnish: ranch salad dressing

Pat pickle slices dry with paper towels; set aside. In a shallow bowl, combine flour and cornmeal; add buttermilk to a separate bowl. Dip pickles into buttermilk, then into flour mixture. In a deep saucepan, heat oil over medium-high heat to 375 degrees. Working in batches, add pickles to hot oil. Fry until golden on both sides, about 3 minutes. Drain on paper towels. Serve warm with ranch dressing for dipping. Serves 8.

Easton's Dill Pickle Dip

Diana Krol
Nickerson, KS

Our grandson Easton considers this yummy dip a special treat!

8-oz. pkg. cream cheese,
    softened
2 c. sour cream

1-1/4 t. garlic salt
5 to 6 whole dill pickles, diced
potato chips

In a serving bowl, stir together cream cheese, sour cream, garlic salt and pickles. Thin to desired consistency with a small amount of pickle juice. Cover and chill overnight. Serve with potato chips. Makes 8 to 10 servings.

Sprinkle pumpkin pie spice inside your Jack-o'-Lantern. When the candle is lit, it will smell heavenly.

Green Chile Cheesecake

Katie Majeske
Denver, PA

This wonderful appetizer has been much requested...it's always a hit at gatherings! It's very appealing to the eye and tastes just as good as it looks.

1 c. tortilla chips, finely crushed
3 T. butter, melted
2 8-oz. pkgs. cream cheese, softened
2 eggs, beaten
1/4 t. chili powder
1/8 t. ground cumin
4-oz. can diced green chiles
1 jalapeño pepper, seeded and chopped

1 c. shredded Colby Jack cheese
1-1/2 c. shredded sharp Cheddar cheese, divided
1 c. sour cream
2 roma tomatoes, chopped
2 to 4 green onions, chopped
3.8-oz. can sliced black olives, drained
Garnish: chopped fresh cilantro tortilla chips

In a bowl, combine crushed chips and butter. Mix well; press into the bottom of an ungreased 9" round springform pan. Bake for 15 minutes; cool slightly and refrigerate until cooled completely. In a separate large bowl, blend cream cheese, eggs and seasonings with an electric mixer on low speed. Add chiles, jalapeño pepper, Colby Jack cheese and one cup Cheddar cheese; blend with mixer. Pour mixture into baked crust. Bake at 325 degrees for 30 minutes; do not overbake. Cool for 10 minutes. Run a knife around edge of pan. Let cool to room temperature. Spread with sour cream; top with remaining Cheddar cheese and vegetables. Cover and chill at least 2 hours. Remove sides of pan and sprinkle with cilantro; serve with tortilla chips. May be prepared up to one day in advance. Serves 12 to 16.

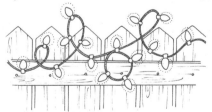

Light the way to your Halloween party magically...
wind twinkling lights of orange and white through the trees,
bushes and around the porch railings.

GAME DAY
Get-Together

Roasted Vegetable Tart

Kristin Stone
Little Elm, TX

We used to live near a fabulous farmers' market where I loved shopping for fresh veggies. My husband doesn't like vegetables as much as I do, so I had to find a way to make them appealing to him. This tart is gorgeous and tastes amazing...he ate it right up!

1 eggplant, peeled and thickly
   sliced
salt to taste
1 red pepper, very thinly sliced
2 zucchini, sliced
1 to 3 tomatoes, sliced

1 T. olive oil
2 t. garlic, minced
dried basil, salt and pepper
   to taste
10 to 12 sheets phyllo dough

Sprinkle eggplant with salt. Let stand for 30 minutes; quickly rinse salt off and drain well. Cut eggplant into one-inch cubes; combine with remaining vegetables in a bowl. Add oil, garlic and seasonings; toss to coat well. Spread vegetables in a single layer on an aluminum foil-lined rimmed baking sheet. Bake at at 450 degrees for 25 to 30 minutes, until tender and any moisture is gone, stirring often. Set aside. Place a sheet of phyllo dough in a 9" pie plate sprayed with non-stick vegetable spray. Spray dough; top with another sheet of dough, rotating slightly to cover sides of pie plate. Add remaining sheets of dough, spraying between sheets. Spoon roasted vegetables into crust; fold sides of crust over vegetables. Reduce oven to 350 degrees. Bake for 25 minutes, or until crust is golden. Cut into wedges. Serves 6.

Make some autumn leaf coasters...so handy for get-togethers!
Cut thick craft felt into leaf shapes, using real leaves as a pattern
or simply cutting free-hand. A stack of coasters tied with
colorful twine would be a nice hostess gift.

Thanksgiving Mini Muffins

Andrea Heyart
Aubrey, TX

These whimsical little bites are such a cute way to serve your Thanksgiving leftovers. They make a perfect appetizer while watching the game or decorating for the holidays...a filling snack after a long day of shopping too!

2 c. leftover stuffing
1 c. roast turkey, diced or
    shredded
1/2 c. turkey gravy

1 egg, lightly beaten
2 c. mashed potatoes
Optional: 1/4 c. cranberry sauce

Combine stuffing, turkey, gravy and egg in a large bowl. Mix together, using your hands or a large spoon. Form into 24 balls; press into paper-lined mini muffin cups. Bake at 350 degrees for 10 minutes. Spoon or pipe mashed potatoes on top of each muffin. Return to oven for an additional 15 to 20 minutes, until heated through. Just before serving, garnish each with 1/4 teaspoon cranberry sauce, if desired. Makes 2 dozen.

Choose a crisp fall evening to host a bonfire party. Gather friends of all ages. Serve chili and hot cider, roast hot dogs, sing songs together and tell ghost stories...every hometown has a few! You'll be making memories that will last a lifetime.

Ham & Cream Cheese Tarts

Sue Klapper
Muskego, WI

Refrigerated biscuits make these quick to prepare. Enjoy!

3/4 c. cream cheese, softened
1 T. milk
1/4 t. orange zest
1/4 t. dry mustard
1/2 c. cooked ham, diced

1/2 c. sour cream dip with chives
12-oz. tube refrigerated biscuits, halved
Garnish: paprika

In a bowl, blend cream cheese, milk, orange zest and mustard. Fold in ham and dip; set aside. Press each biscuit half into an ungreased mini muffin cup. Spoon one tablespoon filling into each cup; sprinkle with paprika. Bake at 375 degrees for 20 to 25 minutes, until golden. Serve warm. Makes about 20 tarts.

A front door wreath offers a warm welcome any time of year. Top off a simple grapevine wreath with autumn bounty...bittersweet vines, lady apples, yarrow, ribbon and raffia.

Scrumptious Spinach Balls

Jennifer Faulkner
Rocky Point, NY

We always make these little treats while watching the Thanksgiving Day parade on TV. They freeze very well...if they aren't eaten up right away! Reheat in the toaster oven for about 5 minutes.

6 eggs, beaten
1 c. butter, melted and slightly
   cooled
1/2 c. grated Parmesan cheese
1 onion, minced

1 clove garlic, minced
2 10-oz. pkgs. frozen chopped
   spinach, thawed and drained
2 c. herb-flavored stuffing mix

In a large bowl, whisk together eggs, butter, cheese, onion and garlic. Add spinach and mix well. Add stuffing and blend well. If mixture is too moist, add a little more stuffing. Roll into walnut-size balls; arrange on lightly greased sheets. Bake at 350 degrees for 20 to 25 minutes, until crisp and golden. Makes 5 dozen.

Keep bottles of soda pop frosty in a metal pail sporting home-team colors...it's easy to make! Rub the pail with steel wool and add the team colors using enamel paint. Let dry overnight, then top with an acrylic spray sealer.

GAME DAY
Get-Together

Shrimp-Stuffed Mushrooms

Mary Smith
Somers, CT

When I was a new wife and mother with no idea how to go about entertaining for the holidays, a dear friend took me under her wing. This is a recipe she shared with me.

6-oz. pkg. pork-flavored
    stuffing mix
1/2 lb. uncooked shrimp, peeled,
    cleaned and finely chopped

20 mushroom caps
1/2 c. butter, divided
8-oz. pkg. shredded mozzarella
    cheese

Prepare stuffing mix according to package directions; cool completely. Mix shrimp with stuffing. Form into small balls; stuff into mushroom caps. Place mushroom caps in an ungreased 13"x9" baking pan; top each with a very thin pat of butter. Dice remaining butter and scatter around mushrooms. Cover with aluminum foil. Bake at 400 degrees for 40 minutes. Uncover; sprinkle mushrooms with cheese and return to oven until cheese melts, about 5 to 8 minutes. Serves 8 to 10.

For a tasty twist on stuffed mushrooms, spoon a favorite stuffed mushroom filling onto wedges of yellow or red pepper. Bake as usual.

Petite Calzones

Carolyn Deckard
Bedford, IN

*My grandkids always want me to fix these when they sleep over.
I do, because I want them to be happy!*

1 c. ricotta cheese
1/2 c. shredded mozzarella
   cheese
1/4 c. shredded Parmesan cheese

10-oz. tube refrigerated flaky
   biscuits
20 very thin slices pepperoni

Combine cheeses in a small bowl and mix well. Split each biscuit horizontally, forming 20 thin biscuits. For each calzone, gently shape one piece of dough into a 4-inch by 2-1/2 inch oval. Top with a pepperoni slice, slightly off-center, and one level tablespoon cheese mixture. Moisten edges with a little water. Fold dough over to enclose filling; pinch edges carefully to seal. Arrange on a lightly greased baking sheet. Bake at 350 degrees for 30 minutes. Serves 4 to 5.

Are lots of kids coming for an after-game party? Make it easy with do-it-yourself tacos or mini pizzas...guests can add their own favorite toppings. Round out the menu with pitchers of soft drinks and a yummy dessert. Simple and fun!

Little Piggies

Kendra Hull
Sterling, IL

This is the perfect finger food for kids! We were going to a party for the big game, and I wanted something yummy that my little boys would enjoy eating. I serve with hot mustard for the "big" people.

2 8-oz. tubes refrigerated
 crescent rolls
14-oz. pkg. mini smoked
 sausages

Optional: favorite mustard

Unroll one tube of crescent rolls and separate into 4 rectangles. Pinch seams together; cut each rectangle into 4 strips. Place a sausage on each strip and roll up. Pinch seams together; arrange seam-side down on an ungreased baking sheet. Bake at 350 degrees for 10 to 12 minutes, until golden. Serve with mustard, if desired. Serves 12.

Sweet-Tart Franks

Carolyn Deckard
Bedford, IN

This is a super-easy dish to take to any kind of party...everyone seems to like them. You can use cocktail weenies too. Be sure to get out the fancy toothpicks!

16-oz. jar mustard
10-oz. jar currant jelly

2 lbs. hot dogs, cut into 1-inch
 pieces

In a microwave-safe 3-quart casserole dish, combine mustard and jelly. Microwave on high setting for 2 minutes. Stir until smooth. Add hot dogs, stirring to coat well. Cover; microwave on high setting for 6 minutes, or until hot dogs are hot. Serves 8.

Light candles for a soft glow
at party time...tuck them into
hollowed-out apples.

Versatile Herb Dip Mix

Kristi Heinz
Chicago, IL

*This is one of the best dip mix recipes I've found...everyone loves it!
I often make large batches, measuring ingredients by 1/2 cupfuls
instead of teaspoonfuls, so I can toss together a delicious dip for
veggies or chips at a moment's notice. It's even good in a crescent roll
veggie pizza! For a nice little gift, I also fill small bags with
5 teaspoons of mix and add the directions. It's a real keeper!*

1 t. dried, minced onion
1 t. dill weed
1 t. dried parsley

1 t. garlic salt
1 t. flavor enhancer

Mix all ingredients in a small plastic zipping bag. Attach directions.
Makes 5 teaspoons mix.

Directions: Add herb mix to one cup sour cream and one cup
mayonnaise. For best flavor, cover and chill overnight. Makes
2 cups dip.

Pack dips and sauces in mini Mason jars to take along to
autumn picnics. Veggie slices and pretzel sticks are easy to dip
right into the jars...and everyone gets their own jar!

No-Guilt Mexican Dip

Anna Hessel
Franklin Park, IL

A delicious dip for guests to enjoy at just about any kind of get-together!

16-oz. container low-fat sour cream
1-oz. pkg. onion soup mix
4 green onions, chopped
1 T. white onion, chopped
2 T. black olives, well drained and chopped
1/4 c. green pepper, chopped
4 t. low-fat mayonnaise
Optional: green onion stems baked tortilla chips, cut-up vegetables

In a serving bowl, blend sour cream with soup mix, stirring until completely mixed. Fold in onions and olives, mixing well. Stir in green pepper until well coated. Add mayonnaise; continue to stir until well blended. Cover and chill until serving time. If desired, garnish by criss-crossing green onion stems along sides of bowl. Serve with tortilla chips and cut-up vegetables. Makes 10 servings.

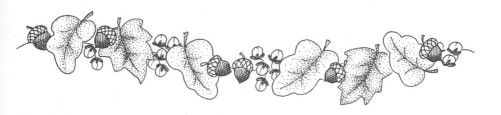

Choose the prettiest leaves to preserve for crafting and decorating. Arrange leaves in a flat pan and cover with a mixture of one part glycerin and two parts water. Use a rock to keep the leaves submerged for one week, then remove and blot dry with paper towels...they'll retain their brilliant colors all season long.

Bite-Size Cranberry Meatballs

Nancy Diem
East Earl, PA

These meatballs are so easy to make and so much fun to eat!

2 lb. ground beef
6-oz. pkg. stuffing mix with
   cranberries
2 eggs, beaten

1 c. water
16-oz. bottle barbecue sauce
14-oz. can whole-berry cranberry
   sauce

In a large bowl, mix together beef, stuffing mix, eggs and water.
Form into 48 small meatballs. Arrange meatballs on a lightly greased
15"x10" jelly-roll pan. Bake at 400 degrees for 16 minutes, or until beef
is no longer pink. Meanwhile, in a saucepan over medium heat, bring
barbecue sauce and cranberry sauce to a boil; mix well. Add meatballs
to sauce mixture; stir to coat evenly. Simmer for several minutes, until
well blended. Makes about 4 dozen.

In harvest time, harvest folk, servants and all
Should make, all together, good cheer in the hall.
–Thomas Tusser

GAME DAY
Get-Together

Chestnut & Bacon Bites

Joyce Borrill
Utica, NY

I've never met anyone who didn't love these crunchy,
smoky-tasting little morsels.

1 lb. bacon
2 to 3 8-oz. cans whole water
   chestnuts, drained

1 c. catsup
1 c. brown sugar, packed

Cut each bacon slice into thirds. Wrap a piece of bacon around each water chestnut. Secure with a toothpick; place on an ungreased baking sheet. Mix catsup and brown sugar in a small bowl; spoon over chestnuts. Bake at 350 degrees for 50 to 60 minutes, until bacon is crisp. Drain on paper towels. Makes about 4 dozen.

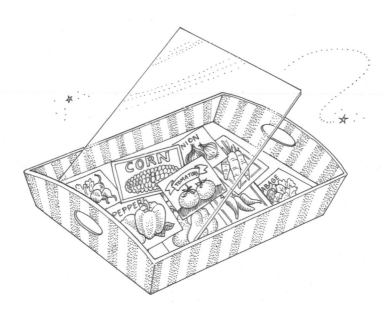

Look for old postcards of your hometown at flea markets and antique shops. They're very inexpensive and such fun to spread out on a table top or serving tray! Cover them with a protective piece of glass cut to fit or arrange them in a large picture frame.

Buttery Onion Pretzels

Sandi Rose
Mansfield, OH

When I made these pretzels for our family's Halloween party, everyone raved about them. As my brother John was leaving, he asked me if he could take some home. I went to get a bag for him and he said, "No, just put a handful in a napkin so I can eat them on the way home!" These really should come with a warning...you can't eat just one!

16-oz. pkg. hard sourdough
   pretzels, broken into
   bite-size pieces

1-1/4 c. butter, sliced
1-oz. pkg. onion soup mix

Put pretzel pieces in a large bowl; set aside. In a small saucepan over low heat, melt butter and add soup mix; stir until heated and well mixed. Pour mixture over pretzels and toss to coat. Spread pretzel mixture in a single layer on an ungreased 15"x10" jelly-roll pan. Bake at 250 degrees for one hour, tossing every 15 minutes. Cool and store in an airtight container. Makes about 10 servings.

Ranch Cayenne Pretzels

Ashley Compoli
Ontario, Canada

This is a big request at my house, especially around the holidays. Everyone usually ends up taking a goody bag home! If you're going to serve these to children, leave out the cayenne pepper. For a different flavor, substitute Italian dressing mix...it tastes wonderful too.

1 c. oil
1-oz. pkg. ranch salad dressing
   mix

1 t. garlic salt
1-1/2 t. cayenne pepper
2 14-oz. pkgs. pretzel sticks

In a bowl, combine oil, dressing mix and seasonings. Divide pretzels between 2 ungreased 15"x10" jelly-roll pans. Drizzle oil mixture over pretzels and stir to coat. Bake at 200 degrees for 1-1/4 to 1-1/2 hours, until golden, stirring occasionally. Cool completely; store in an airtight container. Makes about 10 servings.

Reed's Savory Snack Mix

Jodi Yerges
Watertown, WI

*When my grandson Reed comes over to visit,
this is one of his favorite snacks.*

12-oz. pkg. bite-size crispy corn
& rice cereal squares
1 c. mini pretzel twists
3/4 c. fish-shaped crackers or
other mini crackers
1/2 c. cashews

1/2 c. canola oil
1-oz. pkg. buttermilk ranch
salad dressing mix
1/4 t. lemon pepper
1/2 t. dill weed
1/2 t. garlic powder

In a large roasting pan, combine cereal, pretzels, crackers and cashews; toss to mix and set aside. Combine remaining ingredients in a small bowl; mix well and drizzle over cereal mixture. Stir well to coat. Bake, uncovered, at 250 degrees for 12 minutes. Stir well; bake for an additional 12 minutes. Cool completely; store in an airtight container. Makes about 14 cups.

Share chills and thrills with a monster movie night. Make a
big batch of a favorite snack mix, let the kids each invite
a special friend and scatter plump cushions on the floor
for extra seating. Sure to be fun for everyone!

Candy Apple Crunch

Regina Ferrigno
Gooseberry Patch

Looking for a Halloween treat? This one is no trick to make!

9 c. bite-size crispy corn, rice
   and/or wheat cereal squares
1 c. pecan halves
1/2 c. red cinnamon candies
1/4 c. sugar

1/4 c. butter
1/4 c. water
1 c. dried apple pieces, coarsely
   chopped
cinnamon to taste

In a large bowl, mix cereals and pecans; set aside. In a large heavy saucepan over medium heat, combine candies, sugar, butter and water. Cook, stirring often, until melted and well blended. Pour over cereal mixture; stir until evenly coated. Spread mixture in an ungreased large roasting pan. Bake, uncovered, at 300 degrees for 20 minutes. Stir in apple pieces. Bake an additional 15 minutes. Spread on wax paper to cool, about 20 minutes. Sprinkle with cinnamon. Store in an airtight container. Makes 10 cups.

Pick up some cello treat bags when you shop for baking supplies.
Filled with crunchy treats, tied with curling ribbons and
placed in a basket, they make welcome gifts
to keep on hand for visitors.

Harvest Cashew Popcorn

Hollie Moots
Marysville, OH

I first made this recipe for guests to take home after our housewarming party. It soon became one of my most-requested treats! It's perfect for gifting and yummy for game-time snacking.

6 qts. popped popcorn	1 c. honey
3 c. cashews	2 c. creamy peanut butter
2 c. sugar	1 t. vanilla extract
1 c. light corn syrup	

In a large bowl or roasting pan, combine popcorn and cashews; set aside. In a large heavy saucepan, combine sugar, corn syrup and honey; stir. Bring to a rapid boil over medium heat; boil for 2 minutes. Remove from heat. Add peanut butter and vanilla; stir until smooth. Pour over popcorn mixture; stir to coat. Pour out onto lightly greased baking sheets to cool. Store in an airtight container. Makes about 30 cups.

Show kids how Grandma & Grandpa used to make popcorn, in an old-fashioned hand-cranked popper on the stovetop. They'll love it!

Bewitching Brew

Beth Bundy
Long Prairie, MN

An autumn favorite at our house...this spooky brew is the best!

3 qts. apple cider
1/2 c. brown sugar, packed
6 4-inch cinnamon sticks
1 t. whole cloves

1 t. whole allspice
1/8 t. nutmeg
1/4 t. salt
Optional: orange slices

Combine all ingredients except orange slices in a stockpot. Bring to a boil over medium heat. Reduce heat to low; cover and simmer 20 minutes. Strain to remove whole spices. Serve in mugs; top each mug with an orange slice, if desired. Makes 3 quarts.

For a touch of whimsy on a Halloween buffet, carve a large pumpkin with two different faces, one on each side. Set your Jack-o'-Lantern on a lazy susan and place a lighted candle inside. Now & then, give the lazy susan a twirl. Guests will wonder if they're seeing things!

GAME DAY
Get-Together

Hot Buttered Cider

Judy Lange
Imperial, PA

So good to serve to the girls when we get together to make cookies, or an evening get-together with friends. So so yummy!

1/4 c. butter, softened
1/2 c. brown sugar, packed
1/4 c. honey
1/4 t. cinnamon

1/4 t. nutmeg
3 qts. apple cider
Garnish: cinnamon sticks

In a bowl, beat together butter, brown sugar, honey and spices until well blended and fluffy. Cover; keep refrigerated up to 2 weeks. To serve, bring butter mixture to room temperature. Heat cider in a large saucepan until hot. Fill individual mugs with cider; stir in one tablespoon of butter mixture per mug. Garnish mugs with a cinnamon stick stirrer. Makes 3 quarts.

Clever drink stirrers make hot beverages special. Besides tried & true cinnamon sticks, try cinnamon-flavored candy sticks, bright-colored sticks of rock candy and even sugar cane swizzle sticks.

Harvest Slush

Lisa Robason
Corpus Christi, TX

In South Texas, we don't usually start getting cooler weather until almost Halloween...sometimes we need a refreshing autumn beverage to keep us cool! Good for a warm Midwestern Indian Summer day too.

12-oz. can frozen lemonade
  concentrate
12-oz. can frozen limeade
  concentrate
1 t. orange extract

3 to 4 drops orange food coloring
1 c. powdered sugar
8 c. crushed ice, divided
33-oz. bottle club soda, chilled

In a large bowl, mix lemonade, limeade, extract, food coloring and powdered sugar. Pour half of lemonade mixture into a blender; add 4 cups crushed ice. Blend until slushy. Pour into a large freezer-safe container. Repeat with remaining lemonade mixture and ice; add to freezer container. Cover and freeze until firm. About 30 minutes before serving, remove from freezer and allow to thaw. Transfer to a punch bowl, breaking up any frozen chunks. Pour in club soda; serve immediately. Makes 3 quarts.

Add a spooky mist by filling small black cauldrons with dry ice and a little hot water. Line them up on a table and surround with flickering votives. (Be safe...always wear gloves when handling dry ice.)

PUMPKIN PATCH
Sweets

Apple Bread & Butter Pudding

Teree Lay
Sonora, CA

My grandmother used to share this memory with us. Every New England autumn, she would climb the fence into an abandoned apple orchard to pick apples for her lovely desserts. One year, the orchard was sold without her knowing it. She climbed the fence with her basket, as usual. While singing and picking, she was startled by a man's loud voice saying, "Hey there, just what do you think you're doing?" My grandmother replied in her sweet little voice, "Putting them back!" This memory is still very alive in my thoughts as each harvest season arrives and makes me chuckle to think about it.

1 c. plus 1 T. sugar, divided
3/8 t. cinnamon, divided
5 T. butter, softened and divided
4 Granny Smith or Gravenstein
    apples, peeled, cored and
    sliced

8 slices firm white bread
2 eggs, beaten
1/2 c. milk
1/4 t. vanilla extract

Combine one tablespoon sugar and 1/4 teaspoon cinnamon in a cup; set aside. In a large skillet, melt 4 tablespoons butter over medium-high heat. Add apples and 1/2 cup sugar. Cook, stirring occasionally, until golden, about 25 minutes. Spread one side of each bread slice with remaining butter. Arrange half the bread in the bottom of a 1-1/2 quart casserole dish, butter-side up. Cut remaining slices into 2 triangles each. Spoon apples over bread in pan; arrange triangles around the edge. In a bowl, whisk together eggs and remaining sugar until light; beat in milk, vanilla and remaining cinnamon. Pour egg mixture over apples; let stand 10 minutes. Sprinkle with reserved cinnamon-sugar. Bake, uncovered, at 325 degrees for about one hour, or until golden around the edges and custard is set. Serves 8.

PUMPKIN PATCH
Sweets

Nutmeg Dessert Sauce

Tyson Ann Trecannelli
Gettysburg, PA

This incredible sauce can turn even the most ordinary dessert into a gourmet palate pleaser. I've served it on everything from bread pudding, pumpkin bread and pound cake to baked apples, apple cake and ice cream...you name it! Everyone always wants more. It stores beautifully in the fridge for at least a couple weeks and can be warmed in the microwave as needed.

1 c. sugar	2 c. water
2 T. all-purpose flour	1 T. butter
1/2 t. nutmeg	1 T. cider vinegar

In a saucepan over medium heat, combine sugar, flour and nutmeg. Add water; bring to a boil. Boil for 5 minutes, stirring constantly. Remove from heat; stir in butter and vinegar. Serve warm. May be refrigerated in a covered container up to 2 weeks; rewarm at serving time. Makes about 2-1/2 cups.

Mix up some autumn potpourri. Combine nature-walk finds like pine cones, seed pods and nuts with whole cloves, allspice berries and cinnamon sticks from the spice rack. Toss with a little cinnamon essential oil and display in a shallow decorative bowl.

Maple Custard Pie

Gary-Lee Gordon
Olathe, KS

This recipe makes me think of my grandmother, who always made fall family get-togethers special. When this pie's aroma fills the house, you know in your heart that fall is here! If you can't find maple sugar, substitute one cup light brown sugar plus 1/4 teaspoon maple flavoring.

2 c. milk, divided
1 c. maple sugar, packed
2 T. butter
1 T. cornstarch

3 eggs, beaten
1/2 t. salt
2 9-inch pie crusts
Garnish: nutmeg to taste

Heat 1-1/2 cups milk just to boiling; set aside. In a saucepan over medium heat, cook and stir maple sugar and butter until bubbly. Add the heated milk; stir until sugar is dissolved. Mix in remaining milk, cornstarch, eggs and salt. Pour into unbaked pie crusts; sprinkle with nutmeg. Bake at 450 degrees for 10 minutes; reduce heat to 350 degrees. Continue to bake for 25 minutes, or until a knife inserted in the center comes out clean. Let cool before slicing. Makes 2 pies; each serves 6 to 8.

Beautify your pie! Roll out extra pie crust dough, cut with leaf-shaped mini cookie cutters and press onto the top crust before baking. Or bake cut-outs on a baking sheet at 350 degrees until golden...a fun topper for any kind of creamy pie.

PUMPKIN PATCH
Sweets

~~~~~~~~~~~~~~~~~~~~~~~~~~~~~~~~~~~~~~~

Sweet Potato Cheesecake Pie

Linda Vogt
North Las Vegas, NV

*A dear friend, who knows how much I love to bake in autumn,
sent me this recipe. It has become a favorite with my family &
friends...it's a good thing that the recipe makes three pies!*

1 sweet potato, peeled, cooked
 and mashed
8-oz. pkg. cream cheese,
 softened
1/2 c. plus 2 T. sweetened
 condensed milk

2 eggs, beaten
3/4 c. sugar
3/4 c. brown sugar, packed
1 t. vanilla extract
3 9-inch graham cracker crusts

In a bowl, stir together all ingredients except crusts. Pour into crusts.
Bake at 375 degrees for 55 minutes, or until golden. Cool before slicing.
Makes 3 pies; each serves 6 to 8.

Cherry Buckle Cake

Vicki Nordin
Springfield, IL

*For as long as I've lived, I remember my mother making this cake.
It was the last thing she ever baked for us. Recently I made it for
the first time, and it tasted just like hers...wonderful!*

6 T. butter, sliced
1 c. all-purpose flour
1 c. sugar, divided
2 t. baking powder

3/4 c. milk
14-1/2 oz. can tart red cherries,
 drained and juice reserved

Place butter in a 9"x9" glass baking pan; melt in a 350-degree oven. In
a bowl, combine flour, 1/3 cup sugar, baking powder and milk; stir well.
Pour batter into melted butter in pan. Sprinkle cherries evenly over
batter. Sprinkle remaining sugar over top; drizzle with reserved cherry
juice. Bake at 350 degrees for one hour, or until golden. Serves 8.

Dad's Apple Cake

Sally Hines
Old Forge, PA

This cake was a favorite of my late father-in-law, and I named it in his honor. Dad came to visit us every Sunday evening, and I always had something to satisfy his sweet tooth. In autumn he would go to the local orchard and bring a bag full of apples to our house. This is one of the treats I made for him...the recipe even won me a prize from my local newspaper!

4 c. McIntosh or Macoun apples,
   peeled, cored and cubed
2 c. sugar
1 c. oil
2 t. vanilla extract
2 t. cinnamon
1/2 t. salt

1 c. raisins
1-1/2 c. hot water
3 eggs, beaten
3 c. all-purpose flour
2 t. baking soda
1 c. chopped walnuts

In a large bowl, mix together apples, sugar, oil, vanilla, cinnamon and salt. Let stand for one hour. In a small bowl, cover raisins with hot water; let stand for 10 minutes and drain well. Add raisins to apple mixture along with remaining ingredients. Stir well; pour into a greased 13"x9" baking pan. Bake at 350 degrees for 45 minutes, or until a knife inserted in the center tests clean. Cut into squares. Serves 12 to 15.

Autumn is time for apple fun. Pick your own apples in an orchard, watch cider being pressed at a cider mill or go to a small-town apple butter stirring. Don't forget to taste!

134

PUMPKIN PATCH
Sweets

Memaw's Pear Bundt Cake

Betty Lou Wright
Hendersonville, TN

Decades ago, my mother-in-law used to make this moist, delicious cake during the holiday season. I still treasure her handwritten recipe card. When she died, my aunt took over the job of baking the cake, and now I feel the two of them beside me whenever my kitchen fills with the so-good smells of pears and cinnamon.

2 c. sugar
3 eggs, beaten
1-1/2 c. oil
3 c. all-purpose flour
1 t. baking soda

1 t. salt
1 t. vanilla extract
2 t. cinnamon
3 c. Bartlett pears, peeled, cored
   and thinly sliced

In a large bowl, combine sugar, eggs and oil; beat well. In a separate bowl, mix flour, baking soda and salt. Add flour mixture to sugar mixture, one cup at a time, mixing well after each addition. Stir in remaining ingredients. Spoon batter into a well greased 10" Bundt® pan. Bake at 350 degrees for one hour, or until a toothpick tests done. Turn cake out of pan onto a plate; cool. Drizzle with Powdered Sugar Glaze. Makes 16 servings.

Powdered Sugar Glaze:

1-1/2 c. powdered sugar

2 to 3 T. milk

Stir together ingredients, adding milk to a drizzling consistency.

Create a charming cake stand with thrift-store finds. Attach a pretty plate with epoxy glue to a short glass vase or candle stand for a base. Let dry completely before using...so clever!

Raspberry-Almond Kuchen

Connie Litfin
Carrollton, TX

I make this dessert all year 'round. It has been a family favorite for over 30 years. It is pretty enough for company or a holiday brunch.

1 egg, beaten
1/2 c. milk
1/2 c. sugar
2 T. oil
1 t. almond extract

1 c. all-purpose flour
2 t. baking powder
1 c. fresh raspberries
1/2 c. sliced almonds

In a large bowl, combine egg, milk, sugar, oil and extract. Add flour and baking powder; mix well. Spread batter in a greased 8"x8" baking pan. Sprinkle raspberries, Crumb Topping and almonds over batter. Bake at 375 degrees for 25 to 30 minutes. Cut into squares; serve warm. Makes 9 servings.

Crumb Topping:

3/4 c. all-purpose flour
1/2 c. sugar

3 T. chilled butter

Mix flour and sugar; cut in butter with a fork until crumbly.

Ask Mom to spend an afternoon showing you how to make the delicious dessert she's always been famous for. Be sure to have a pad & pen handy to write down every step and a camera to take some snapshots. Afterwards, sample it together along with cups of steamy hot tea or coffee.

Cranberry-Orange Pear Pie

Debbie Blundi
Kunkletown, PA

I created this light and tasty pie for the hearty Italian pasta meals my husband's family enjoys. It's perfect for our church's Sunday potluck luncheons too.

1 c. sweetened dried cranberries,
   chopped
1-1/2 c. orange juice
9-inch deep-dish pie crust
1/3 c. sugar

1/4 c. all-purpose flour
1 t. pumpkin pie spice
2 24-oz. cans diced pears,
   drained

Combine cranberries and orange juice in a bowl. Refrigerate for several hours to overnight; drain. Bake pie crust at 350 degrees until lightly golden, about 15 minutes. Meanwhile, in a large bowl, mix sugar, flour and spice; add pears and cranberries. Pour into crust. Spread Streusel Topping evenly over pie. Bake at 350 degrees until golden, 30 to 40 minutes. Makes 6 to 8 servings.

Streusel Topping:

1 c. all-purpose flour
1/2 c. brown sugar, packed

1 t. orange extract
1/2 c. chilled butter

Mix together all ingredients with a fork until crumbly.

Scoop up small tart tins at antique shops...they make the sweetest bite-size pies!

Buttermilk Fry Cakes

Alysson Marshall
Clifton Springs, NY

My Aunt Delores always made these yummy doughnuts on Halloween for my grandmother's birthday party. We enjoyed them with hot mulled apple cider. Now I love to make them in the fall for my family because of the memories they bring back.

2 eggs, beaten
1 c. buttermilk
1 c. sugar
1/4 c. oil
1 t. vanilla extract
4 c. all-purpose flour

1 T. baking powder
1/4 t. baking soda
1/2 t. salt
oil for deep frying
Garnish: powdered sugar or
  cinnamon-sugar

In a large bowl, whisk together eggs, buttermilk, sugar, oil and vanilla. In a separate bowl, mix flour, baking powder, baking soda and salt. Add flour mixture to egg mixture; stir well. Cover and refrigerate for one hour. Roll out dough 1/2-inch thick on a lightly floured surface. Cut with a 3-inch doughnut cutter. In a deep large saucepan over medium-high heat, heat several inches of oil to 375 degrees. Fry doughnuts, a few at a time, turning once. Drain on paper towels. Dip in powdered sugar or cinnamon-sugar; serve warm. Makes one dozen.

Whip up a tasty apple cider glaze for doughnuts. Mix up 2-1/2 cups powdered sugar and 1-1/2 teaspoons apple pie spice. Stir in 1/4 cup apple cider until a drizzling consistency is reached.

Walnut-Raisin Baked Apples

Melissa Olson
Brooklyn, NY

A wonderful fall dessert for two to share!

2 Fuji, Gala or Granny Smith
   apples
2 T. raisins

1/4 c. chopped walnuts
2 T. maple syrup
1 T. butter, diced

Core apples with a knife. Make a 3/4-inch wide cavity in the center of each apple, stopping 1/2 inch from the bottom. Pare the top inch of apples. Place apples in a baking pan. Fill with raisins and walnuts; drizzle with maple syrup and top with butter. Bake, uncovered, at 350 degrees until tender, 45 to 60 minutes. Let cool 5 to 10 minutes before serving. Serves 2.

Mini Apple Turnovers

Robyn Stroh
Calera, AL

One day I needed a dessert to take to my church's women's club but was short on time. So I created this recipe...it was a hit!

2 9-inch pie crusts
21-oz. can apple pie filling

1 egg white
1 T. water

Place one pie crust on a lightly floured surface. With a 3-inch biscuit cutter, cut out as many as circles as possible. Top each circle with one to 2 teaspoons pie filling, cutting apples into smaller pieces as necessary. Fold circles in half; crimp the edges with a fork dipped in water. Place on lightly greased baking sheets. Repeat with second crust. In a small bowl, beat together egg white and water until slightly foamy; brush over turnovers. Bake at 425 degrees for 8 to 12 minutes, until golden. Makes one to 1-1/4 dozen.

Maple-Nut Snacking Loaf

Kelley Nicholson
Gooseberry Patch

*One loaf to enjoy, one to share! Serve with cream cheese
for a real treat.*

21-oz. can apple pie filling
12-oz. can evaporated milk
3 eggs, lightly beaten
1/2 c. butter, melted
1 T. maple flavoring
3 c. all-purpose flour
1 c. whole-wheat flour

1-1/3 c. brown sugar, packed
3/4 c. wheat bran cereal
1/2 c. chopped walnuts
2 t. baking soda
2 t. salt
2 t. cinnamon

Place apple filling in a large bowl; chop apples slightly. Add milk, eggs, butter and flavoring. In a separate large bowl, stir together remaining ingredients. Add apple mixture to flour mixture; stir just until moistened. Divide batter between 2 greased 8"x4" loaf pans. Bake at 350 degrees for 55 to 65 minutes, until a toothpick inserted in the center tests clean. Cool in pans on a wire rack for 10 minutes. Turn loaves out onto rack; cool completely. Makes 2 loaves.

Thanksgiving is a perfect time to send a thank-you note to a favorite teacher, coach or scout leader telling them how much they mean to you. Let them know what you're doing now and include a photo...they're sure to be pleased to hear from you.

Butternut Squash Pie

Carol Baize
Canton, OH

*This pie always makes me think of harvest time and Thanksgiving.
Fresh squash is very flavorful, but if you're short on time,
frozen puréed squash is convenient.*

1 butternut squash, halved
   lengthwise and seeds
   removed
2 to 4 T. butter, sliced
1 c. evaporated milk
1/2 c. sugar
1 T. all-purpose flour

1/2 t. ground ginger
1/2 t. nutmeg
1/2 t. cinnamon
1/2 t. salt
2 eggs, beaten
9-inch pie crust
Garnish: whipped topping

Place squash halves in a shallow baking pan, cut-side up. Top with butter; cover with aluminum foil. Bake at 375 degrees for about one hour, until fork-tender. Remove from oven; turn squash halves on their side in the pan and allow liquid to drain until cool. Scoop squash pulp into a bowl and mash, discarding skin. Measure 1-1/2 cups of mashed squash into the top of a double boiler; add milk and warm through over low heat. In a separate bowl, mix sugar, flour, spices and salt; add eggs. Whisk well; add to squash mixture and stir well. Warm through, but do not boil. Pour warm filling into unbaked pie crust. Bake at 400 degrees for 10 minutes. Reduce heat to 350 degrees; bake until pie sets, about 15 to 20 minutes. Top servings with a dollop of whipped topping. Serves 6.

An old hometown tradition was "Never return a dish empty."
After Thanksgiving, gather up casserole dishes and pie plates
that have been left behind, fill them with homebaked
goodies and return to their owners!

Fresh Apple Pound Cake

Theresia King
Knoxville, TN

My Great-Aunt Kathleen gave me this recipe. She is no longer with us, but I always think of her when I bake this cake.

1-1/4 c. oil
2 c. sugar
3 eggs
2 t. vanilla extract
3 c. all-purpose flour

1 t. baking soda
1 t. salt
3/4 t. cinnamon
3 apples, peeled, cored and diced
1 c. chopped pecans

Combine oil, sugar and eggs in a bowl. Beat with an electric mixer on medium speed for 3 minutes; beat in vanilla. In a separate bowl, combine flour, baking soda, salt and cinnamon; mix well. Add flour mixture to oil mixture. Beat well; fold in apples and pecans. Pour batter into a greased 12" Bundt® pan. Bake at 350 degrees for one hour and 20 minutes, or until a toothpick tests done. Cool for several minutes; turn cake out of pan. Serves 16.

An old-fashioned cake walk is still fun today! Played like musical chairs, each person stands in front of a number placed on the floor. When the music stops, a number is called out... whoever is standing nearest that number gets to take his or her pick of the baked goodies.

PUMPKIN PATCH
Sweets

Coffee Can Pumpkin Cake

Sandie Rivet
Johnsonville, NY

Round slices of this delicious cake look so pretty on dessert plates, topped with a dollop of whipped cream and a sprinkle of nutmeg. It freezes well...what a handy make-ahead idea!

2 c. pumpkin
1 c. oil
4 eggs, beaten
2/3 c. water
3-1/2 c. all-purpose flour
2-1/2 c. sugar

2 t. baking powder
1 t. nutmeg
1 t. cinnamon
Optional: 1 c. raisins,
    1/2 c. chopped walnuts

In a large bowl, whisk together pumpkin, oil, eggs and water. In a separate large bowl, combine flour, sugar, baking powder and spices. Add flour mixture to pumpkin mixture; stir well. Fold in raisins and walnuts, if using. Spoon batter into 4 well greased 16-ounce metal cans or 5-1/2"x3" mini loaf pans, filling half-full. Place on a baking sheet. Bake at 350 degrees for one hour and 10 minutes, or until cakes test done when a toothpick is inserted in center. Cool in cans on a wire rack for 20 minutes. Run a knife around the edges; turn cakes out of cans. Makes 4 mini loaves.

Line a vintage pail with a cheery tea towel and tuck in freshly baked mini loaves of sweet bread...add several sample-size jars of jam too!

Lake Norden School
Chocolate Cake

Stephanie Carlson
Sioux Falls, SD

This wonderful chocolate cake was the favorite of every student at Lake Norden Elementary by far! Getting a piece of cake meant having to eat ALL of your lunch. Lunch could've been nothing but Brussels sprouts, but we still would've cleaned our plates for a piece of this cake!

2-1/2 c. all-purpose flour
2 c. sugar
1/4 c. baking cocoa
1 T. baking soda
1 c. oil
1 c. buttermilk

2 eggs, room temperature and
   lightly beaten
1/8 t. salt
1 c. boiling water
1 t. vanilla extract
Garnish: favorite frosting

In a bowl, combine flour, sugar, cocoa and baking soda. Sift together 3 times; set aside. In a separate bowl, mix oil, buttermilk, eggs and salt. Add flour mixture to oil mixture; mix well. Add boiling water and vanilla; stir until thoroughly combined. Pour into a greased 13"x9" baking pan. Bake at 325 degrees for 40 to 45 minutes, until a toothpick inserted in the center tests clean. Cool; spread with frosting and cut into squares. Serves 12 to 15.

String dried Chinese lantern flowers to dress up a mantel for fall. Their bright orange color really brings the autumn colors inside!

Triple Layer Mud Pie

Beth Williamson
Wakefield, RI

I will always remember this pie because I made it for my mother the last time I saw her. She loved it! We shared a last Thanksgiving together in 2008...she passed away just a few months later.

3 sqs. semi-sweet baking
   chocolate, melted
1/4 c. sweetened condensed milk
9-inch chocolate cookie crust
1/2 c. pecans, toasted and
   chopped

2 c. milk
2 3.9-oz. pkgs. instant chocolate
   pudding mix
8-oz. container frozen whipped
   topping, thawed and divided

In a bowl, stir together melted chocolate and condensed milk; pour into crust. Sprinkle with pecans. Combine milk and dry pudding mixes in a bowl; whisk together for 2 minutes. Spoon 1-1/2 cups of pudding over pecans; set aside. Stir half of whipped topping into remaining pudding; spread over layer in crust. Top with remaining topping. Cover and chill until serving time. Makes 6 servings.

Invite friends over for an address-the-Christmas-cards party...the week after Thanksgiving would be perfect. Ask them to bring their cards, stamps, address books and address stickers. You provide a dessert, beverages and some holiday music. You'll all be done in no time!

Ada's Prune Spice Cake

Linda Barker
Mount Pleasant, TN

My Aunt Ada was a terrific cook! This old-fashioned cake was one of her specialties. It's wonderfully spicy and so moist.

1 c. prunes
1-1/2 c. sugar
1 c. oil
3 eggs, beaten
1 t. vanilla extract
2 c. all-purpose flour
1 t. baking soda

1/2 t. salt
1 t. cinnamon
1 t. allspice
1 t. nutmeg
1 c. buttermilk
1 c. black walnuts or other nuts, chopped

In a saucepan, cover prunes with water. Cook over medium heat until tender; drain. Cool and chop prunes; set aside. In a large bowl, beat together sugar, oil, eggs and vanilla. In a separate bowl, sift together flour, baking soda, salt and spices. Add flour mixture and buttermilk alternately to sugar mixture; stir well. Fold in prunes and nuts. Pour batter into a greased 10" tube pan. Bake at 350 degrees for 40 minutes, or until cake tests done with a toothpick. Pour hot Butter Sauce over cake while cake is still in pan; turn out of pan and cool. Makes 10 servings.

Butter Sauce:

1/2 c. butter
1 c. sugar

1/3 c. buttermilk
1 T. light corn syrup

Mix all ingredients in a saucepan. Bring to a boil over medium heat.

Enjoy a relaxing holiday season...make treats ahead of time and freeze them for gifts and last-minute occasions. Freeze baked, unfrosted cookies up to 6 months, pies up to 4 months and quick breads up to 3 months. Be sure they are wrapped tightly, labeled and dated.

Arlene's Apple Crisp Pie

Delores McKinnie
Long Beach, MS

I learned about this recipe from a woman who, with her husband, owned an orchard in Three Rivers, Michigan. Back in the 1980s, my husband and I worked there picking apples, cherries and peaches. Arlene would bake this wonderful pie to share with us workers. I have made it myself ever since.

1 egg
1/4 c. water
1 T. vinegar
1 t. vanilla extract
3 c. all-purpose flour
3 c. butter-flavored shortening
3/4 c. plus 1 T. sugar, divided
1 t. salt

6 Golden Delicious apples, peeled, cored and sliced
1/2 t. cinnamon
1/4 t. nutmeg
5 T. butter, sliced
1/4 c. whipping cream
Garnish: French vanilla ice cream

In a large bowl, beat together egg, water, vinegar and vanilla; set aside. In a separate bowl, mix together flour, shortening, one tablespoon sugar and salt. Add flour mixture to egg mixture; stir until a soft dough forms. Divide dough into 2 balls. Roll out dough, one ball at a time, to 10-inch circles on a floured surface. Place one crust into a 9" pie plate. Arrange apple slices in crust. Sprinkle with remaining sugar and spices; dot with butter and drizzle with cream. Add top crust; seal and trim edges. Make 3 slits in top crust to vent. Bake at 350 degrees for 20 minutes. Sprinkle with Crisp Topping. Bake at 350 degrees for an additional 30 to 40 minutes. Serve warm, topped with ice cream. Makes 8 servings.

Crisp Topping:

3/4 c. all-purpose flour
1/3 c. chilled butter

1/2 c. brown sugar, packed
1/4 T. cinnamon

Mix all ingredients together with a fork until crumbly.

Jazz up homemade apple desserts in a jiffy. Top with a drizzle of warm caramel sauce...scrumptious!

Harvest Peach-Berry Cobbler ▶

Lori Ritchey
Denver, PA

*I just love this peach cobbler! Cranberries and orange zest
give it a little extra zing.*

2/3 c. butter, melted
15.6-oz. pkg. cranberry quick
   bread & muffin mix
2 29-oz. cans sliced peaches,
   drained and 1 c. syrup
   reserved
1 egg, beaten

2 T. orange zest, divided
1/2 to 2/3 c. sweetened dried
   cranberries
1/3 c. sugar
1 T. cinnamon
Garnish: whipped cream or
   vanilla ice cream

Spread melted butter in a 13"x9" baking pan; set aside. In a large bowl,
combine dry bread mix, reserved peach syrup, egg and one tablespoon
orange zest. Stir until moistened. Drop batter by heaping spoonfuls over
melted butter; spread slightly without stirring. Arrange peaches over
batter; sprinkle with cranberries. In a small bowl, combine sugar,
remaining zest and cinnamon; mix well and sprinkle over fruit. Bake at
375 degrees for 50 to 60 minutes, until edges are deeply golden. Cool
slightly; dollop individual servings with whipped cream or ice cream.
Serves 12.

Heap high the board with plenteous cheer
and gather to the feast,
And toast the sturdy Pilgrim band
whose courage never ceased.

–Alice W. Brotherton

Simple Pear Cobbler

Gloria Warren
Ontario, Canada

This quick & easy dessert is just wonderful on a fall day. I especially love to bake it after picking fresh pears. Try using several different kinds of pears like Anjou and Bosc...yummy!

5 c. ripe pears, peeled, cored
    and thinly sliced
1 T. self-rising flour
1 c. sugar
1/8 t. ground ginger

3/4 c. water
1/4 c. butter, sliced
9-inch pie crust
Optional: ice cream

Spread pears in a lightly greased 10"x10" baking pan. Mix together flour, sugar and ginger in a small bowl; sprinkle over pears. Pour water evenly over pears. Dot with butter. Place crust on top; cut several slits in crust to vent. Place on lower rack of oven. Bake at 375 degrees for 40 to 45 minutes. Serve warm, topped with ice cream if desired. Makes 8 to 10 servings.

For plump, juicy raisins or dried cranberries, cover them with boiling water and let stand for 15 minutes. Drain and pat dry with a paper towel before adding to a dessert recipe.

Frozen Vanilla Decadence

Beverly Mahorney
Cynthiana, KY

Whatever the occasion, if there's a potluck coming up, everyone expects me to bring a dessert! This scrumptious ice cream treat is my own creation, equally good for tailgating and Thanksgiving.

2 c. graham cracker crumbs
1/4 c. butter, melted
1/3 c. sugar
14-oz. can sweetened condensed milk
2 3.4-oz. pkgs. instant French vanilla pudding mix
1 qt. vanilla ice cream, softened

2 c. salted peanuts, chopped and divided
1 c. toffee baking bits, divided
1 c. fudge ice cream topping, divided
8-oz. container frozen whipped topping, thawed

In a bowl, mix graham cracker crumbs, melted butter and sugar. Press into an ungreased 13"x9" baking pan. In a separate bowl, mix condensed milk, dry pudding mixes and softened ice cream. Spread over crumb layer; sprinkle with one cup peanuts and 1/2 cup toffee bits. Drizzle with 1/2 cup fudge topping. Spread with whipped topping; add remaining peanuts, toffee bits and fudge topping. Cover and freeze until firm. Soften slightly to serve; cut into squares. Makes 12 servings.

Spiderweb cupcakes for Halloween! Frost cupcakes, then pipe concentric circles with frosting in a different color. Pull a toothpick through the frosting while it's still wet.
Try it on full-size layer cakes too.

Mom's Pink Cranberry Freeze

Molly Wilson
Rapid City, SD

I grew up in Texas where it gets quite hot, so whenever we had any sort of get-together, church social or family reunion, my mom was always asked to make this frozen treat. It's a refreshingly different cranberry dessert for the holidays too.

1-1/2 c. cream cheese, softened
1/4 c. mayonnaise
1/4 c. sugar
2 14-oz. cans whole-berry
   cranberry sauce
20-oz. can crushed pineapple,
   drained

1 c. chopped pecans, walnuts
   or almonds
2 c. whipping cream
1 c. powdered sugar
2 t. vanilla extract

In a large bowl, blend cream cheese, mayonnaise and sugar. Fold in fruit and nuts; set aside. In a deep bowl, beat whipping cream with an electric mixer on high speed until soft peaks form. Stir in powdered sugar and vanilla. Fold whipped cream mixture into cream cheese mixture. Spoon into several loaf pans or a large deep dish. Cover and freeze for at least 6 hours before serving. Serves 25.

Old-time penny candy is fun for kids of all ages! Fill vintage apothecary jars with a variety of candies...gumdrops, licorice, caramels, sour balls, root beer barrels, peppermints and lemon drops. Set out several filled jars and let everyone choose their favorites.

Gingered Hazelnut Cookies

Brenda Melancon
McComb, MS

I love ginger cookies, ginger cake, ginger anything! One day I was craving something sweet and gingery, and these delectable cookies were the outcome. I hope you'll love them too.

2/3 c. butter, softened
3-oz. pkg. cream cheese,
   softened
17-1/2 oz. pkg. sugar cookie mix
1/2 c. cake flour
1/4 t. baking soda
1 egg, beaten

1 t. maple flavoring
1/3 c. crystallized ginger,
   finely diced
1/2 c. hazelnuts, toasted
   and chopped
1/2 c. granola cereal with
   dates or raisins

In a large bowl, combine butter and cream cheese. Beat with an electric mixer on medium speed until light and fluffy. Add dry cookie mix; beat on low speed until moistened. Add cake flour, baking soda, egg and flavoring. Beat on low speed until combined. Stir in remaining ingredients. Drop by tablespoonfuls, 2 inches apart, onto baking sheets lightly coated with non-stick vegetable spray. Bake at 350 degrees for 11 to 13 minutes, until lightly golden. Cool cookies on baking sheets for 2 minutes; remove to wire racks and cool completely. Makes 4 dozen.

Homemade goodies being mailed to faraway friends are a double treat when wrapped in familiar hometown newspapers.

No-Bake Maple Cookies

Janis Parr
Ontario, Canada

These yummy little cookies don't need to be baked and are ready in a jiffy. They disappear as fast as I can make them!

2 c. brown sugar, packed
1/2 c. milk
1/2 c. butter
1 T. vanilla extract

2 t. maple syrup
3 c. long-cooking oats, uncooked
1 c. sweetened flaked coconut

Combine brown sugar, milk and butter in a large saucepan over medium-high heat. Bring to a boil; boil for 3 minutes, stirring constantly. Remove from heat. Add remaining ingredients, stirring well to mix. Drop by rounded tablespoonfuls onto wax paper. Allow to cool. Store cookies in an airtight container, using wax paper to separate the layers. Makes 3 dozen.

Whimsical vintage aprons are easily found at thrift shops and tag sales. Start your own collection to hang from pegs! Everyone can tie on their own ruffled, polka-dotted or flowered favorite whenever they help out in the kitchen.

Leslie's Gingersnaps

Leslie McCullough
Liberty Township, OH

These spicy cookies are an autumn favorite in our home...just right with a mug of hot tea or mulled cider!

4 c. all-purpose flour
1 T. baking soda
1/2 t. salt
2 t. ground cloves
2 t. ground ginger
2 t. cinnamon

1-1/2 c. shortening
2 c. sugar
2 eggs, beaten
1/2 c. molasses
Garnish: additional sugar

In a bowl, combine flour, baking soda, salt and spices; set aside. In a separate large bowl, blend together shortening and sugar until light and fluffy. Add eggs and molasses; beat until fluffy. Add flour mixture slowly to shortening mixture; stir thoroughly. Roll into balls by tablespoonfuls; coat balls in sugar. Place on ungreased baking sheets; do not flatten. Bake at 375 degrees for 10 to 14 minutes, to desired crispness. Cool on wire racks. Makes 5 dozen.

Take a hayride to the pumpkin patch! Pack a picnic, pull on a sweater and spend a lazy afternoon with your family enjoying the colors of fall and picking out the perfect pumpkin.

Vermont Maple Cookies

Joan White
Malvern, PA

These cookies are soft, chewy and deliciously buttery. I use Grade A maple syrup, but for more maple flavor, you can use Grade B syrup. I sometimes use crushed walnuts sprinkled on top...the crunch of walnuts gives them real personality.

3/4 c. butter
1/2 c. brown sugar, packed
1 egg, beaten
1 t. vanilla extract
2-1/4 c. all-purpose flour
1/2 t. baking powder

1/2 t. baking soda
1/2 t. salt
1/2 c. maple syrup
1/2 c. chopped walnuts
Garnish: walnut halves

In a large bowl, blend butter and sugar. Beat in egg and vanilla; set aside. In a separate bowl, mix together flour, baking powder, baking soda and salt; add to butter mixture alternately with maple syrup. Blend well and fold in chopped walnuts. Drop dough onto ungreased baking sheets, 2 tablespoons dough per cookie. Top each cookie with a walnut half. Bake at 400 degrees for 8 to 10 minutes. Cool on wire racks. Drizzle Maple Glaze over cooled cookies. Makes 3 dozen.

Maple Glaze:

1/4 c. powdered sugar   4 t. maple syrup

Mix together ingredients until smooth.

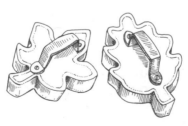

Autumn leaf cookies are fun to make! Divide your favorite sugar cookie dough into three or four bowls and mix a few drops of red, yellow or orange food coloring into each bowl. Roll dough out separately, cut with leaf-shaped cookie cutters and bake.

Crisp Chewy Oat Cookies

Beverly Daugherty
Upper Arlington, OH

I've been baking these cookies since I was ten...that's over 50 years!
They have a fantastic aroma and taste like autumn to us.

1-1/2 c. all-purpose flour
1 c. sugar
1 t. baking soda
1/2 t. salt
1/2 t. ground cloves
1/2 t. ground ginger

3/4 c. butter, softened
1 egg, beaten
1/4 c. dark molasses
3/4 c. quick-cooking oats,
   uncooked

In a bowl, mix together flour, sugar, baking soda, salt and spices. Add butter, egg and molasses. With an electric mixer on medium speed, beat until smooth, about 2 minutes. Stir in oats. Drop dough by level tablespoonfuls, 2 inches apart, onto ungreased baking sheets. Bake at 375 degrees for 8 to 10 minutes; do not overbake. Cool on baking sheets for 2 minutes; remove to a wire rack with a wide spatula. Store in an airtight container. Makes 3-1/2 dozen.

Pumpkin Spice Shortbread

Judy Young
Plano, TX

When I was growing up in England, my mother used to make
shortbread all the time. It just melts in your mouth!

1 c. butter, softened
1/2 c. powdered sugar
2 c. all-purpose flour

3/4 t. pumpkin pie spice
Optional: nutmeg to taste
Garnish: sugar

In a bowl, blend butter and powdered sugar. In a separate bowl, mix flour and spices; add to butter mixture and stir well. Turn dough out onto an ungreased baking sheet. Pat into a 7-inch circle, 3/4-inch thick. Smooth edge; decorate edge with the tines of a fork. Pierce all over with fork. Chill at least 30 minutes. Bake at 375 degrees for 5 minutes. Reduce oven to 300 degrees. Bake for another 45 minutes, or until lightly golden. While still warm, cut into 8 to 16 wedges; sprinkle with sugar. Cool on baking sheet; store in an airtight container. Makes 8 to 16 wedges.

PUMPKIN PATCH
Sweets

Old-Fashioned Soft Pumpkin Cookies ▶

Lisa Ann Panzino DiNunzio
Vineland, NJ

These cookies are so soft and cake-like...they will disappear quickly!
They're delicious either with or without the glaze.

2-1/2 c. all-purpose flour
1 t. baking powder
1 t. baking soda
1/2 t. salt
1 t. cinnamon
1/2 t. nutmeg
1/2 c. butter, softened

1-1/2 c. sugar
1 c. canned pumpkin
1 egg, beaten
1 t. vanilla extract
1 T. maple syrup
Optional: colored sugar,
　　candy sprinkles

In a bowl, mix flour, baking powder, baking soda, salt and spices; set aside. In a large bowl, beat butter and sugar until well blended. Beat in pumpkin, egg, vanilla and maple syrup until smooth. Gradually beat in flour mixture. Drop by rounded tablespoonfuls onto greased baking sheets. Bake at 350 degrees for 14 to 17 minutes, until edges are firm. Cool on baking sheets for 2 minutes; remove to wire racks and cool completely. Drizzle Vanilla Glaze over cookies. Decorate with colored sugar or sprinkles, if desired. Makes about 3 dozen.

Vanilla Glaze:

2 c. powdered sugar
3 T. milk

1 T. butter, melted
1 t. vanilla extract

Combine all ingredients; stir until smooth.

A terrific party favor...jumbo cookies tucked into paper CD envelopes from the office supply store. Decorate the envelopes with stickers or rubber stamps. Your guests will thank you!

English Toffee Cookie Bars

Sue Rae Stevenson
Sheboygan, WI

A lovely take-along dessert...I'm always asked for the recipe!

1 c. butter, softened
1 c. brown sugar, packed
1 egg yolk
1 t. vanilla extract

2 c. all-purpose flour
8 1-1/2 oz. milk chocolate candy
    bars, broken into pieces
1 c. chopped walnuts

In a bowl, blend butter and brown sugar. Add egg yolk and vanilla; mix well. Add flour; mix well. Pat dough into a sheet in an ungreased 15"x10" jelly-roll pan. Bake at 350 degrees for about 18 to 20 minutes, until edges are lightly golden. Remove from oven; immediately place chocolate pieces on top. When chocolate is melted, spread with a spatula, like frosting. Sprinkle with chopped nuts. Cut into squares. Makes 2-1/2 dozen.

If you love salty-sweet flavors, try sprinkling a pinch of
flaky sea salt over your favorite melted chocolate or
caramel confections...yum!

S'Morelicious Cookies

Isabelle Sampson
Nova Scotia, Canada

My grandchildren love making s'mores in the summertime, then eating until they rub their bellies and say, "I think I had too many!" So I thought I'd make these easy cookies for them to enjoy all year 'round... they're a hit!

1 c. butter
1 c. brown sugar, packed
1/2 c. sugar
2 eggs, beaten
1-1/2 t. vanilla extract
1-1/2 c. all-purpose flour
1-1/2 c. whole-wheat flour
1-1/2 t. baking soda

1/2 t. salt
2/3 c. mini semi-sweet
    chocolate chips
1 c. cinnamon graham crackers,
    crushed
1 c. mini marshmallows
Optional: 1 c. semi-sweet
    chocolate chips, melted

Combine butter and sugars in a large bowl. With an electric mixer on low speed, beat until light and fluffy. Add eggs and vanilla; beat until smooth. In a separate bowl, mix flours, baking soda and salt; add to butter mixture. Beat with mixer on low; gradually increase to medium and beat well. Add chocolate chips, cracker crumbs and marshmallows; mix well with your hands. Form into large palm-size balls. Place balls on parchment paper-lined baking sheets, 2 to 3 inches apart. Bake at 375 degrees for 15 minutes, or until just turning golden. Cool slightly; remove to wire racks and cool completely. If desired, swirl melted chocolate over cooled cookies. Makes about 16 jumbo cookies.

Give your fireplace a welcoming autumn glow...fill it with several pots of flame-colored orange and yellow chrysanthemums.

Game-Day S'Mores Bars

Paula Marchesi
Lenhartsville, PA

*We love football and my entire family looks forward to every game.
I really enjoy preparing all sorts of scrumptious goodies for us.
These cookie bars are the next best thing to campfire s'mores.
Mmm...delicious!*

1/2 c. butter, softened
3/4 c. sugar
1 egg, beaten
1 t. vanilla extract
1-1/3 c. all-purpose flour
3/4 c. graham cracker crumbs

1 t. baking powder
1/4 t. salt
4 1-1/2 oz. milk chocolate
   candy bars
1 c. marshmallow creme

In a large bowl, beat butter and sugar with an electric mixer on medium speed until creamy. Add egg and vanilla; beat until combined. In a small bowl, combine flour, cracker crumbs, baking powder and salt. Add to butter mixture; beat until combined. Press half of dough evenly into a lightly greased 8"x8" baking pan. Lay chocolate bars over dough, breaking apart as needed to create an even layer. Spread marshmallow creme over chocolate. Spread remaining dough on top. Bake at 350 degrees for 30 to 35 minutes. Cool slightly. Cut into bars; serve warm. Makes 2 dozen.

Sunny fall days are ideal for bulb planting...that's when you'll find the best selection at garden centers too. Why not get together with neighbors to plant everyone's bulbs? Afterwards, share homemade cookies fresh from the oven and hot cider.

SLOW-COOKER
Potluck Pleasers

Scrambled Eggs for a Crowd

JoAnn

*A foolproof recipe for a tailgating brunch! You can even
speed it up by prepping all the ingredients the night before
and tucking them into the fridge.*

2 doz. eggs
1 c. half-and-half
1/2 t. salt
1/2 t. pepper
2 c. cooked ham, diced

1 T. butter
1/2 c. red pepper, chopped
1/2 c. green onions, chopped
1/2 c. sliced mushrooms
1 c. shredded Cheddar cheese

In a large bowl, whisk together eggs, half-and-half and seasonings.
Spray a slow cooker with non-stick vegetable spray; pour mixture into
slow cooker. Top with ham. Cover and cook on high setting for one
hour, stirring after 30 minutes. Cover and cook an additional 40 to
50 minutes, stirring every 10 minutes, until eggs are moist and almost
set. In a skillet, melt butter over medium heat; add vegetables. Sauté for
5 minutes, stirring occasionally, until tender. Fold vegetable mixture
and cheese into eggs. Cover and let stand several minutes, until cheese
melts. Serve immediately, or turn to low setting and hold up to one
hour. Serves 10 to 12.

Slow cookers are super year 'round...no matter what the occasion.
So grab a friend and head out to a local craft show, barn sale
or small-town county fair. When you come home,
a delicious meal will be waiting for you!

Layered Potatoes & Onions

Loretta Mullen
Snellville, GA

My husband must eat gluten-free, so I'm always looking for recipes he can enjoy. These hearty homestyle potatoes are a winner!

3 to 4 lbs. potatoes, thinly sliced
3 to 4 yellow onions, thinly
  sliced
1 c. butter, sliced
salt and pepper to taste
chopped fresh chives to taste

In a slow cooker sprayed with non-stick vegetable spray, layer 1/4 each of the potatoes, onions and butter; add salt, pepper and some chives. Repeat layering, ending with butter and seasonings. Cover and cook on high setting for one hour. Turn slow cooker to low setting; cook for 5 hours more. Serves 10 to 12.

Serve poached eggs with breakfast potatoes or hash. Fill a skillet with water and bring to a simmer. Swirl the water with a spoon and gently slide in an egg from a saucer. Let cook until set, about two minutes, and remove egg with a slotted spoon.

Sausage-Egg Casserole

Ellie Brandel
Clackamas, OR

*This is a terrific breakfast recipe...it can cook overnight while you
sleep and is ready in the morning. The boiling step eliminates
a lot of fat from the sausage, leaving just the great flavor.*

1/2 lb. ground pork breakfast
   sausage
1/4 c. mustard
10 slices white bread
6 eggs, beaten

1-1/2 c. milk
salt and pepper to taste
8-oz. pkg. shredded sharp
   Cheddar cheese

In a skillet over medium heat, cover sausage with water. Boil for
5 minutes; drain well. Continue cooking until sausage is browned,
breaking up with a spatula. Meanwhile, spread mustard on one side of
each bread slice. Cut each slice into 9 squares and place in the bottom
of a lightly greased slow cooker. In a bowl, whisk together eggs, milk,
salt and pepper. Layer cheese and sausage over bread; pour egg mixture
over top. Cover and cook on low setting for 8 hours, or until a knife tip
tests clean. Serves 6 to 8.

Enjoy a weekend retreat at home! Spend the day in your
jammies...savor a leisurely brunch, work puzzles, re-read a
favorite book or browse holiday catalogs. What could be cozier?

Caramel-Pecan Rolls

Nancy Wise
Little Rock, AR

Mmm...my family can't get enough of these sticky rolls!

1/2 c. butter, melted
1 c. brown sugar, packed
1 t. cinnamon

1/4 c. chopped pecans
2 8-oz. tubes refrigerated
    biscuits

Add butter to a small bowl. Combine brown sugar, cinnamon and pecans in a separate small bowl. Dip biscuits into melted butter, then into brown sugar mixture. Arrange biscuits in a greased slow cooker, layering as necessary. Cover and cook on high setting for about 1-1/2 hours. To serve, turn biscuits out onto a plate. Makes 16 servings.

Apple Pie Oatmeal

Nicole Stalnaker
Beverly, MA

On chilly autumn mornings, I love knowing that my family is starting the day with a hearty, comforting bowl of oatmeal.

2-1/2 c. whole milk
1 c. steel-cut oats, uncooked
1 to 2 Granny Smith apples,
    cored and chopped
1/2 c. raisins
1/2 c. chopped walnuts
2 T. brown sugar, packed

2 T. honey
1 T. butter, diced
1 T. ground flax seed
1 T. apple pie spice
1/8 t. salt
Garnish: additional milk,
    brown sugar

Spray a slow cooker with non-stick vegetable spray. Put all ingredients except garnish in slow cooker; stir gently. Cover and cook on low setting for 6 to 8 hours. Top individual servings with milk and brown sugar. Makes about 6 servings.

Turn lengths of burlap into rustic placemats...no sewing required!
Simply cut and fringe the edges.

Chilly-Day Spicy Chicken Soup

Beth Cassinos
Silver Springs, NV

Whenever the first blustery autumn day arrives, this hearty soup is sure to be bubbling in my slow cooker. Be careful not to touch your face after chopping the serranos, they'll bite you!

3 boneless, skinless chicken
   breasts, cooked and shredded
28-oz. can crushed tomatoes
2 14-oz. cans chicken broth
2 c. water
2 to 3 serrano peppers, seeded
   and chopped
1/2 yellow onion, diced

1/4 to 1/2 bunch fresh cilantro,
   chopped
salt and pepper to taste
Optional: 11-oz. can corn,
   drained
Garnish: crushed tortilla chips,
   shredded Cheddar cheese

Add all ingredients except garnish to a large slow cooker; stir. Cover and cook on low setting for 2 hours, or until heated through. If soup is too thick, add a little more water. Serve topped with crushed tortilla chips and cheese. Makes 8 servings.

For whimsical napkin rings, tie ears of red-kerneled strawberry popcorn with a raffia bow and lay on folded napkins.

Stuffed Pepper Soup

Jill Jones
Canal Fulton, OH

*The gentleman who gave us this recipe, Brad, loved to cook.
Our whole church group always looked forward to his cooking,
and this satisfying soup was especially popular. Enjoy!*

2 lbs. lean ground beef
28-oz. can diced tomatoes
28-oz. can tomato sauce
3 c. green peppers, coarsely
    chopped

1/2 c. onion, chopped
1 c. long-cooking rice, uncooked
1/4 c. brown sugar, packed
2 cubes beef bouillon
salt and pepper to taste

In a skillet over medium heat, brown beef; drain. Add beef, tomatoes with liquid and remaining ingredients to a slow cooker; stir. Cover and cook on low setting for 7 to 8 hours. Check rice for doneness; add more water if a thinner consistency is desired. Serves 8.

Save a few seeds from this year's Jack-o'-Lantern to plant next
spring. Air-dry them and tuck into an envelope. They may
produce a true pumpkin, or a squmpkin (a cross between
a squash and a pumpkin)...but that's the fun of it!

Turkey Noodle Soup

Jennie Gist
Gooseberry Patch

There's no need to wait for Thanksgiving leftovers to make this delicious soup! Look for turkey thighs and drumsticks at the butcher's counter early each autumn.

2 lbs. turkey thighs or
   drumsticks
2 carrots, peeled and sliced
2 stalks celery, thinly sliced
1 c. onion, chopped
1 t. garlic, minced
1/2 t. poultry seasoning
4-1/2 c. turkey or chicken broth
1/2 c. fine egg noodles, uncooked
2 T. butter
1/4 c. fresh parsley, chopped
salt and pepper to taste

In a large slow cooker, combine turkey, carrots, celery, onion, garlic and seasoning. Pour in broth. Cover and cook on high setting for 5 hours, or until meat is falling off bones. Remove turkey to a plate; let cool. Stir in noodles; cover and cook an additional 15 to 20 minutes, or until noodles are tender. Meanwhile, cut turkey into bite-size pieces; discard skin and bones. When noodles are done, stir in turkey, butter and parsley; season with salt and pepper. Serves 4.

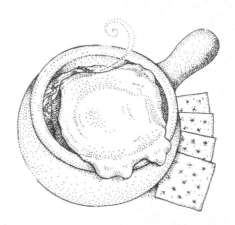

Soup is so nice when shared. Thank a friend with a basket of warm rolls and a pot of steaming homemade soup. What a welcome surprise on a brisk day!

Kansas Corn Chowder

Diana Krol
Nickerson, KS

I've had this recipe for ages...it's quick, easy and just delicious. Perfect with a warm muffin and a crisp salad on an autumn night.

3 slices bacon, diced
1 onion, diced
16-oz. pkg. frozen corn, thawed
1 potato, peeled and chopped
2 c. chicken broth
1 t. salt
1/4 t. pepper
2 c. half-and-half or milk
Optional: 2 T. butter,
   2 T. all-purpose flour
Garnish: nutmeg

In a skillet over medium heat, cook bacon until crisp. Remove bacon, reserving drippings. Sauté onion in drippings until tender. In a slow cooker, combine bacon, onion mixture, vegetables, broth and seasonings; stir well. Cover and cook on low setting for 8 hours. Stir in half-and-half or milk shortly before serving. If a thicker chowder is desired, blend butter with flour. Stir into chowder and cook until thickened. Serve chowder sprinkled with a dash of nutmeg. Makes 6 to 8 servings.

For a quick fall centerpiece, set a spicy-scented orange pillar candle in a shallow dish. Surround with unshelled hazelnuts or acorns...done!

Stuart Family Chili

Tami Kendrick
Herriman, UT

My family always ate this chili on Halloween...something warm, hearty and delicious to keep us trick-or-treating. Now I love to cook it throughout the winter. All my friends love it too!

2 lbs. ground beef or turkey
1 c. onion, chopped
1 c. celery, chopped
1 c. green pepper, chopped
15-1/2 oz. can diced tomatoes
16-oz. can tomato sauce
2 15-1/2 oz. cans red kidney
   beans, drained
1-1/2 c. catsup

1/4 c. brown sugar, packed
1/4 c. lemon juice
2 T. chili powder
2 T. Worcestershire sauce
2 t. ground cumin
1-1/2 t. salt
1/2 t. dry mustard
1 bay leaf

In a skillet over medium heat, brown meat with onion, celery and green pepper; drain. Add meat mixture to a large slow cooker; stir in tomatoes with juice and remaining ingredients. Cover and cook on low setting for 4 to 5 hours. Discard bay leaf before serving. Makes 12 servings.

A hometown chili cook-off! Ask neighbors to bring a pot of their best "secret recipe" chili to share, then have a friendly judging for the best. You provide lots of crackers and buttered cornbread, chilled cider and bright red bandannas for terrific lap-size napkins.

170

Gramma's Beef Barley Soup

Kendall Hale
Lynn, MA

It's terrific to come home and find this savory soup waiting for me! I work long days, so I'm always happy to find a slow-cooker recipe that can cook for 10 to 12 hours.

2 c. carrots, peeled and chopped
1 stalk celery, diced
1/2 green pepper, diced
1/2 c. frozen cut green beans
1/2 c. frozen corn
2 lbs. stew beef cubes
1 onion, chopped
2 to 3 T. oil
16-oz. can stewed tomatoes
2/3 c. pearled barley, uncooked
1 T. beef bouillon granules
1 T. dried parsley
3/4 t. dried basil
2 t. salt
1 t. pepper
5 c. water

Add carrots, celery, green pepper, beans and corn to a large slow cooker; set aside. In a skillet over medium-high heat, brown beef and onion in oil; drain and add to slow cooker. In a bowl, combine tomatoes with liquid, barley, bouillon and seasonings; pour over beef. Add water, filling slow cooker 2/3 full; do not stir. Cover and cook on low setting for 10 to 12 hours. Serves 10 to 12.

A bountiful harvest garland for the mantel...tie ears of Indian corn in bunches, evenly spaced, onto a length of raffia.

Savory Beef & Vegetables

Erin Brock
Charleston, WV

Looking for a crockery roast that isn't made with cream of mushroom soup? Here you are! A chuck roast works well too. If you're pressed for time, don't brown the beef..just fill 'er up and go.

4 potatoes, peeled and cut into
    wedges
4 carrots, peeled and cut into
    1-inch pieces
1 onion, thinly sliced
1 bay leaf
1 T. all-purpose flour
1/2 t. salt

1/8 t. pepper
2 lbs. beef top round, cut into
    serving-size pieces
1 t. Worcestershire sauce
14-1/2 oz. can beef broth,
    divided
2 T. cornstarch

Add potatoes, carrots, onion and bay leaf to a slow cooker sprayed with non-stick vegetable spray; set aside. In a shallow bowl, mix flour, salt and pepper. Add beef pieces; coat well. Spray a skillet with vegetable spray; heat over medium-high heat. Add beef and brown on all sides. Add to slow cooker along with Worcestershire sauce and 1-1/2 cups broth. Refrigerate remaining broth. Cover and cook on low setting for 8 to 10 hours. Remove beef and vegetables to a serving platter; keep warm. Pour liquid from slow cooker into a saucepan; discard bay leaf. In a small bowl, mix remaining broth and cornstarch until smooth; add to liquid in saucepan. Bring to a boil over medium-high heat, stirring constantly. Cook and stir for one minute, or until thickened. Serve pan gravy with beef and vegetables. Serves 4 to 6.

Decorate your dining room table with a sweet table runner.
Purchase two to three yards of cotton fabric in a seasonal print,
then edge with rick rack edging and add a tassel at each end.
So simple, you'll want to make several!

Stuffed Flank Steak

Lisa Sett
Thousand Oaks, CA

This is one of my best slow-cooker recipes...it's easy, delicious and good enough for company! We grow our own blackberries, so I always have blackberry jam on hand, but grape jam and orange marmalade may also be used.

1-1/2 lbs. beef flank steak
1-1/2 c. dry bread crumbs
1/2 c. mushrooms, finely diced
1/4 c. grated Parmesan cheese

1/4 c. beef broth
2 T. butter, melted
2 T. oil

With a sharp knife, score steak lightly on both sides without cutting all the way through. Place a 24-inch length of kitchen twine under steak; set aside. In a bowl, mix together remaining ingredients except oil; spread over steak. Roll up steak; tie with twine. Pour oil into a slow cooker. Add steak; turn to coat on all sides. Spoon Gravy over steak. Cover and cook on low setting for 8 to 10 hours, until tender. Remove steak to a platter. Let stand several minutes; discard twine. Slice steak, using an electric knife, if possible. Serves 6 to 8.

Gravy:

.87-oz. pkg. brown gravy mix
1 c. water
1/4 c. blackberry jam

1/4 c. apple juice
Optional: 2 T. green onion, minced

Combine gravy mix and water in a small saucepan over medium heat. Bring to a boil, stirring frequently. Reduce heat to low; simmer for one minute. Stir in remaining ingredients.

Save the memories! Be sure to take pictures at your harvest gathering and share copies with friends as a thank-you for coming.

Hula Hoop Hawaiian Chicken

Laurie Wilson
Fort Wayne, IN

Serve your family a sweet and savory meal in the fall with a hint of summertime taste. The onions will stay a little crunchy, which I love. This dish tastes wonderful even the next day.

3 T. cornstarch
1 c. chicken broth
3 lbs. boneless, skinless chicken
   thighs
20-oz. can crushed pineapple
1 c. brown sugar, packed

1-oz. pkg. Italian salad dressing
   mix
1/2 red pepper, diced
1 sweet onion, thickly sliced
1 T. soy sauce
cooked rice

In a small bowl, stir cornstarch into broth; set aside. Place chicken in a slow cooker; top with undrained pineapple and remaining ingredients except rice. Add broth mixture; stir gently. Cover and cook on high setting for 4 to 5 hours, stirring once an hour. Serve over rice. Serves 10 to 12.

Mandy's Chicken Delight

Mandy Simons
Ontario, Canada

I have fond memories of the aroma of poultry seasoning whenever my mom roasted a chicken. I created this recipe so I could use my favorite seasoning more often. For a complete meal, place some cubed potatoes and baby carrots in the bottom of the slow cooker and add 1-1/2 cups water. Ta dah...dinner is ready!

3 to 4 chicken breasts or thighs
2 T. butter, softened
2 T. poultry seasoning

1 T. dried rosemary
1/2 c. Italian salad dressing

Place chicken in a slow cooker. Spread chicken with butter; sprinkle evenly with seasonings and drizzle with salad dressing. Cover and cook on high setting for 4 hours, or until juices run clear when chicken is pierced. Serves 3 to 4.

BBQ Chicken Chowdown

Lisa Kastning
Marysville, WA

Our family had so much fun coming up with a name for this delicious, easy recipe! Try adding chopped red or green peppers to the chicken, or even some jalapeño slices for some kick.

4 to 6 boneless, skinless chicken
    breasts
24-oz. bottle barbecue sauce
8-1/2 oz. pkg. cornbread mix
14-1/2 oz. can corn, drained

8-oz. pkg. shredded Cheddar
    cheese
8 to 10 slices bacon, crisply
    cooked and crumbled

Place chicken in a slow cooker; top with barbecue sauce. Cover and cook on low setting for 6 to 7 hours, until chicken shreds easily with 2 forks. Meanwhile, prepare and bake cornbread mix according to package directions; set aside. Shortly before serving time, add corn to slow cooker. Turn to high setting and cook for 15 minutes, or until warmed through. To serve, spoon chicken mixture over squares of cornbread; top with cheese and bacon. Serves 4 to 6.

Enjoy a girls' day out. Meet friends at a favorite café or diner where you can count on the food to be delicious and homemade. Settle in and spend the afternoon together chatting and catching up on each other's families and upcoming plans...such fun!

Turkey & Mushroom Sauce

Sandy Wise
Skaneateles, NY

Early in January, several friends of mine would gather to celebrate the coming of another new year. Our host provided the main course and everyone else brought the sides. This dish was exceptional...I wouldn't have guessed he made it in a slow cooker!

4 to 5-lb. turkey breast
2 T. butter, melted
1/4 c. sherry or chicken broth
2 T. fresh parsley, chopped

1/4 t. dried tarragon
paprika to taste
1/2 t. salt
1/4 t. white pepper

Place turkey, skin-side up, in a large slow cooker. Brush with butter; sprinkle with sherry or broth and seasonings. Cover and cook on high setting for one hour; reduce to low setting and cook for 6 to 7 hours, until center reads 165 degrees on a meat thermometer. Remove turkey to a platter; cover loosely and set aside. Strain drippings from slow cooker and spoon off any fat; reserve drippings to make Mushroom Sauce. Slice turkey and serve with Mushroom Sauce. Makes 8 to 10 servings.

Mushroom Sauce:

reserved turkey drippings
2-1/2 oz. can sliced mushrooms,
    drained
2 T. cornstarch

1/4 c. sherry or chicken broth
1/4 t. dried tarragon
salt and pepper to taste

Place drippings in a 2-cup glass measuring cup. Add mushrooms and enough water to measure 1-3/4 cups; set aside. Dissolve cornstarch in sherry or broth and stir into drippings. Pour into a small saucepan; add seasonings. Cook and stir over medium heat until thickened; keep warm.

Turn pressed-glass jelly jars into charming votive holders. Add sparkling coarse salt to each and nestle a votive inside. Line up several jars down the center of the table.

Cranberry Pork Roast

Charlene Boice
Lake City, FL

We love to make this recipe for family and company,
especially in autumn. It's delicious and so simple.

3-lb. rolled boneless pork loin
   roast
14-oz. can jellied cranberry sauce
1/2 c. cranberry juice
1/2 c. sugar

1 t. mustard
1/4 t. ground cloves
2 T. cornstarch
2 T. cold water
salt to taste

Place roast in a large slow cooker; set aside. Mash cranberry sauce in a bowl; stir in cranberry juice, sugar and seasonings. Pour mixture over roast. Cover and cook on low setting for 6 to 8 hours, until tender. Remove roast to a platter; keep warm. Skim fat from liquid in slow cooker and measure 2 cups, adding water if necessary. Pour into a saucepan; bring to a boil over medium heat. In a small bowl, combine cornstarch and cold water to make a paste. Stir into hot mixture in saucepan. Cook and stir until thickened. Season with salt. Serve gravy with sliced pork. Serves 6 to 8.

Get everyone outdoors for a little fresh air after Thanksgiving dinner...try pumpkin bowling! Simply roll pumpkins toward two-liter bottles filled with water. Sure to be a hit with kids of all ages!

Sweet-and-Sour Pork Roast

Wendy Lee Paffenroth
Pine Island, NY

It's terrific to walk in after a hard day at work and have a wonderful meal to sit down to. Serve with a baked potato and a green salad with some crusty rolls...mmm good!

2 c. baby carrots
1 head cabbage, coarsely
   shredded
3-lb. boneless pork roast

1/2 c. brown sugar, packed
1/4 c. cider vinegar
2 12-oz. cans ginger ale
1/2 c. jellied cranberry sauce

Add carrots to a large slow cooker; top with cabbage, then pork. In a small bowl, mix together brown sugar and vinegar; spoon over pork. Add ginger ale to slow cooker. Cover and cook on low setting for 8 to 9 hours, or on high setting for 5 to 6 hours, until pork is fork-tender. Remove pork to a platter; keep warm. Add cranberry sauce to a small microwave-safe bowl and microwave about one minute; drizzle over pork. Serve sliced pork with carrots and cabbage. Serves 4 to 6.

October gave a party;
The leaves by hundreds came.
The chestnuts, oaks and maples,
And leaves of every name.

–George Cooper

Pork Chile Verde Burritos

Donna Butler
Barstow, CA

I don't even know where I got this recipe, but I use it often. I've shared it with friends and they make it over & over too. It's especially enjoyed by men and teens, who even request the leftovers for breakfast!

3-lb. bone-in pork butt roast,
   cut into bite-size pieces
1/2 lb. pork chorizo sausage,
   casing removed and crumbled
29-oz. can pinto beans
16-oz. jar medium or hot salsa
1 onion, chopped
4-oz. can diced green chiles

2 T. jalapeño peppers, seeded
   and chopped
2 to 3 cloves garlic, pressed
2 doz. 10-inch flour tortillas,
   warmed
16-oz. pkg. shredded Monterey
   Jack or Cheddar cheese
Garnish: sour cream

Place meats in a large slow cooker. Add undrained beans, salsa, onion, chiles, jalapeños and garlic. Cover and cook on low setting for 10 to 12 hours, until pork is very tender. To serve, top each tortilla with 1/2 cup pork mixture and a handful of cheese; roll up. Top with another 1/2 cup pork mixture and more cheese. Warm in microwave briefly, until cheese melts. Serve with sour cream. Makes about 20 burritos.

This year, host a Trunk-or-Treat in your church parking lot for little ones. Cars pull into parking spots, then pop their decorated trunks open as little clowns and cowboys, pirates and princesses go from car to car trick-or-treating. Afterwards, bring everyone inside for a warming supper served family style.

BBQ Beef or Pork

Diana O'Connor
Uvalde, TX

*My daughter Delany loves this recipe...it's terrific for all kinds of fall
parties and get-togethers! Serve the shredded meat on hamburger
buns with pickles and onions, or on tortillas with hot sauce.*

4-lb. beef chuck roast or
    pork loin roast
salt and pepper to taste
1 to 2 T. oil
14-oz. bottle catsup
12-oz. can cola

5 T. light brown sugar, packed
1/4 c. applesauce
1/4 c. Worcestershire sauce
1-1/2 T. mustard
hamburger buns or tortillas

Season roast with salt and pepper. Heat oil in a skillet over medium-
high heat; brown roast on all sides. Place roast in a large slow cooker.
Cover and cook on low setting for 6 to 8 hours, until roast is very
tender. Remove roast to a platter; discard juices in slow cooker. Shred
meat with a fork and return to slow cooker. Stir in remaining ingredients
except buns or tortillas; mix well. Cover and cook for an additional
3 hours. Serve shredded meat on buns or tortillas, as desired. Makes
8 servings.

Mini versions of favorite hot sandwiches are so appealing on party
platters...fun for sampling too! Try using small sandwich rolls or
brown & serve dinner rolls instead of full-size buns.

Molasses Baked Beans

Cyndi Little
Whitsett, NC

I'm always looking for good slow-cooker recipes. I love my slow cookers and use them more often than my stove. This recipe was shared with me by a friend and has become a family favorite.

2 16-oz. pkgs. dried navy beans
1/2 to 1 lb. salt pork, cut into
   strips
3/4 to 1-1/4 c. molasses, divided
3/4 c. dark brown sugar, packed
1 T. dry mustard
salt and pepper to taste
2 onions, chopped
1 whole onion
10 whole cloves

Cover beans with water in a large pot; soak for 2 to 3 hours. Drain beans, reserving liquid; place beans in a slow cooker. Add salt pork, 3/4 cup molasses, brown sugar, mustard, salt, pepper and chopped onions. Stud whole onion with cloves; add to slow cooker. Pour in enough of reserved liquid to fill half full; stir. Cover and cook on high setting for 4 to 5 hours, or on low setting for 8 to 9 hours, until beans are tender. After several hours, if a darker color is desired, stir in remaining molasses; continue cooking as directed. Serves 8.

Plenty of ready-to-eat goodies can be found at farmers' markets. Tuck a basket filled with picnic supplies into the car trunk along with a quilt to sit on. Instant picnic!

Brenda's Cream Tacos

Brenda Bailey
Gentry, AR

*I started making this recipe in the 1980s from a recipe I tweaked
when I lived in Texarkana. I have made it for my family, church
socials and many times for work socials. It is so simple and yummy!*

16-oz. pkg. pasteurized process
   cheese, diced
8-oz. container frozen whipped
   topping, thawed
2 15-oz. cans ranch-style beans

2 15-oz. cans chili without
   beans
10-oz. can diced tomatoes with
   green chiles
corn chips

Combine all ingredients except corn chips in a slow cooker; stir. Cover
and cook on low setting for one to 2 hours, until cheese melts. Stir.
Serve spooned over corn chips in small bowls. Makes about
12 servings.

Green Chile Chicken Dip

Holly Child
Parker, CO

*I first tried this recipe at a potluck at work, years & years ago.
I decided to make it and try it out on my boyfriend Jeff, who later
became my husband. To this day, it is still his very favorite treat, and
he makes it for any occasion, big or small.*

12-1/2 oz. can chicken, drained
2 8-oz. pkgs. cream cheese,
   softened and cubed
4-oz. can diced jalapeño peppers

2 4-oz. cans diced green chiles
2 10-3/4 oz. cans cream of
   chicken soup
tortilla chips

In a slow cooker, combine all ingredients except chips; do not drain
peppers or chiles. Stir until well blended. Cover and cook on low setting
for 3 to 4 hours, stirring occasionally. Serve warm with tortilla chips.
Serves 10 to 12.

SLOW-COOKER
Potluck Pleasers

Cheesy Bean Dip

Carmen Hyde
Spencerville, IN

This recipe is a hit at gatherings! Sometimes I add 1/2 pound browned ground beef to make it even heartier. Often when we go camping I'll take along a slow cooker and pop everything in the crock after breakfast...it's ready to enjoy by lunchtime!

8-oz. pkg. cream cheese,
   softened
1 c. sour cream
16-oz. can refried beans
2 T. taco seasoning mix
1-1/2 t. onion powder

8-oz. pkg. shredded Colby Jack
   cheese, divided
nacho-flavored tortilla chips
Garnish: chopped tomatoes,
   sliced black olives, guacamole

In a bowl, blend cream cheese, sour cream, beans and seasonings. In a slow cooker, layer half of cream cheese mixture and half of shredded cheese; repeat layering. Cover and cook on low setting for 4 hours. Serve warm with tortilla chips, garnished as desired. Makes 12 servings.

Show your hometown spirit...cheer on the high school football team with a Friday night block party. Invite neighbors to bring along their favorite appetizer to share and don't forget to wear school colors!

Tangy Pineapple Meatballs

Leslie Nagel
Noxapater, MS

This recipe was given to me by my husband's stepmother, who would serve it as an appetizer before Thanksgiving dinner. Now I make these meatballs often, as they are a big hit! Any leftovers are yummy served on hoagie buns.

40-oz. pkg. frozen meatballs,
    thawed
2 T. oil
16-oz. can pineapple tidbits

24-oz. bottle catsup
1 c. brown sugar, packed
1/2 c. maple syrup
1/4 c. soy sauce

In a skillet over medium heat, brown meatballs in oil. Drain well on paper towels. In a slow cooker, combine pineapple with juice and remaining ingredients; mix well and stir in meatballs. Cover and cook on low setting for 2 to 3 hours. Makes about 20 servings.

Having a Halloween party? Simple, tried & true games are fun for all ages...bobbing for apples, telling ghost stories and visiting the mad scientist's lab, blindfolded, to touch cauliflower "brains" and spaghetti "worms."

Hawaiian Wings

Yvonne Van Brimmer
Apple Valley, CA

I like to bring the taste of the islands to our parties. This simple recipe has no last-minute prep so you can enjoy your friends! Tasty served as an appetizer or over steamed rice for dinner.

4 to 5 lbs. frozen chicken wings, thawed
1 onion, chopped
1/3 c. low-sodium soy sauce
20-oz. can pineapple chunks
granulated garlic to taste
2 t. ground ginger
Optional: shredded coconut

Place wings in a large slow cooker. Top with onion, soy sauce, pineapple with juice, garlic and ginger. Toss gently to coat. Cover and cook on low setting for 8 hours, or until wings are no longer pink in the center. Sprinkle with coconut, if desired. Makes 6 to 8 servings.

Carve an extra Jack-o'-Lantern or two and deliver to elderly neighbors so they can enjoy some Halloween fun... what a neighborly gesture!

Harvest Candied Sweet Potatoes

Julie Pak
Henryetta, OK

My dad grows a big garden, and every fall he always has lots of sweet potatoes. This recipe's ingredients complement each other in a special way...the kids love it! It makes a great side or even dessert.

4 sweet potatoes, peeled and cut
    into 2-inch cubes
2 Granny Smith apples, peeled,
    cored and thickly sliced
1/2 c. golden raisins

1/2 c. butter, sliced
3/4 c. brown sugar, packed
1/2 c. pancake syrup
1/2 t. cinnamon
1/8 t. salt

In a slow cooker, layer half each of sweet potatoes, apples and raisins. Add half each of butter, brown sugar, syrup and seasonings. Repeat layers, ending with seasonings. Cover and cook on low setting for 4 to 6 hours. Serves 6.

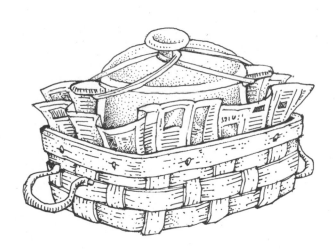

If you're traveling "over the river and through the woods" for the holiday, carry along a slow cooker without spilling. Pull two large rubber bands around the knob on the lid and over the handles. Wrap it in newspaper to hold in the heat, then just plug in the slow cooker when you arrive. Food will stay hot and delicious.

Golden Roasted Veggies

Jen Thomas
Santa Rosa, CA

*I'm always looking for new ways to serve the herbs and veggies
I bring back from the farmers' market. This recipe is very flavorful
and is really simple to fix.*

6 Yukon Gold potatoes, peeled
   and cubed
4 carrots, peeled and sliced
2 parsnips, peeled and sliced
1/4 c. butter, melted

1 T. fresh tarragon, snipped
1 T. fresh sage, snipped
1 t. brown sugar, packed
1/2 t. salt
1/2 t. pepper

Combine all ingredients in a slow cooker. Stir gently to coat vegetables well. Cover and cook on low setting 6 to 8 hours, or on high setting for 3 to 4 hours, until tender. Serves 6 to 8.

Decorate the house in unexpected places...a golden ribbon
around a stack of Shaker boxes, a garland of autumn leaves
around the hallway mirror and even a bow or two on
the backs of the dining room chairs.

Any-Day Mashed Potatoes

Cyndy DeStefano
Mercer, PA

*My family loves mashed potatoes! So I came up with this easy recipe...
the potatoes practically cook themselves. Be sure to add a
big pat of butter at serving time!*

1 lb. baking potatoes, peeled
   and cubed
1/2 c. chicken broth
2 T. butter, sliced
1/4 c. sour cream

1/4 t. garlic powder
1/4 t. salt
1/4 t. pepper
1/4 to 1/2 c. milk, warmed

In a slow cooker, combine potatoes, chicken broth and butter. Cover and
cook on high setting for 4 hours, or until potatoes are tender. Add sour
cream and seasonings. Mash potatoes with a potato masher or an
electric mixer on low speed until well blended. Stir in enough milk for
desired consistency. Cover and keep warm on low setting until serving
time, up to 2 hours. Stir again before serving. Serves 5.

Gourds and mini pumpkins left from Halloween can be put to
charming new use at Thanksgiving. Simply spray them gold
with craft paint to tuck into harvest centerpieces.

Old-Time Sage Dressing

Gert Stevens
Sioux City, IA

Our family came for Thanksgiving dinner each year, and since I have MS, I needed recipes that were easy to prepare. We would mix this dressing the night before, keep it in the fridge, then pop it in the slow cooker early the next morning. The sage flavor reminds me of my mother's dressing from years gone by.

3/4 c. margarine
1 onion, chopped
1 c. celery, chopped
2 16-oz. loaves 2-day-old
   white bread
4 eggs, beaten

2 10-3/4 oz. cans cream of
   chicken soup
1 t. baking powder
1 t. dried sage, or to taste
1/2 t. pepper
14-oz. can chicken broth

Melt margarine in a skillet over medium heat. Add onion and celery; sauté for 10 to 15 minutes. Meanwhile, cube bread to measure 20 cups; place in a large bowl. In a second bowl, whisk together eggs, soup, baking powder and seasonings; stir in broth. Pour onion mixture and egg mixture over bread cubes. Stir until bread is well coated and moistened. Grease a large slow cooker very well. Add mixture to slow cooker. Cover and cook on high setting for one hour. Turn to low setting; continue cooking another 4 to 5 hours. Stir in edges of dressing every 30 to 45 minutes to prevent sticking. More broth may be added during cooking for a moister dressing. Serves 6 to 8.

Try a progressive dinner for Thanksgiving...it's fun and less work for all. Each family serves one course at their house as everyone travels from home to home. Start at the first house for appetizers, move to the next for soups and salads, again for the main dish and end with dessert. Slow cookers keep everything warm and tasty!

Minister's Delight

Marsha Baker
Pioneer, OH

My youth pastor's wife gave me this recipe. It's a scrumptious Sunday dessert that can be left to cook in the slow cooker while you're away at church. Very simple and versatile...change it up to your favorite flavor. Oh-so delicious!

21-oz. can apple, cherry,
   blueberry or peach pie filling
Optional: 1 c. crushed pineapple,
   partially drained
18-oz. pkg. yellow cake mix

1/2 c. butter, melted
Optional: 1/3 c. chopped walnuts
   or pecans
Garnish: ice cream or whipped
   topping

Spray a slow cooker with non-stick vegetable spray. Add pie filling; spread pineapple over top, if using. In a bowl, combine dry cake mix and butter; mix with a fork until crumbly. Sprinkle over pie filling. Sprinkle nuts on top, if desired. Before covering, place 2 paper towels on top of slow cooker to catch any condensation. Cover and cook on low setting for 2 to 3 hours. Serve warm with ice cream or whipped topping. Makes 5 to 6 servings.

Stock up on your favorite nuts in the fall, when they're just-picked. Shelled or unshelled, nuts will stay fresher longer if they're stored in the freezer. As an added benefit, unshelled nuts will crack much easier when frozen.

Baked Lemon Sponge

Cheri Maxwell
Gulf Breeze, FL

A light, lemony dessert...very welcome after a hearty meal!

1 c. sugar
1/4 c. all-purpose flour
1/4 t. salt
1/4 c. lemon juice
1 T. lemon zest

3 eggs, separated
1/2 c. butter, melted
1 c. milk
Garnish: powdered sugar

In a bowl, combine sugar, flour and salt. Stir in lemon juice, zest, egg yolks, butter and milk; set aside. In a separate deep bowl, beat egg whites with an electric mixer on high speed until stiff peaks form. Gently fold egg whites into lemon mixture. Pour into a lightly greased heat-proof bowl that fits into a slow cooker; cover tightly with aluminum foil. Set bowl in slow cooker; carefully pour in water to one inch up sides of bowl. Cover and cook on high setting for 4 to 5 hours, until fluffy and set. Dust with powdered sugar. Serves 4.

Invert a glass garden cloche and fill it with mini gourds, nuts and interesting seed pods. Top with a tray and turn right-side up for a pretty display on a mantel or sideboard.

Hot Caramel Apple Cider

Kimberly Hancock
Murrieta, CA

A perfect warmer-upper for a chilly fall day. Put the cider on to simmer, go out for a hayride or an afternoon of apple picking, and when you get home the scent of this cider will have filled the whole house! What could be better?

1/2 gal. apple cider
1/2 c. brown sugar, packed
1-1/2 t. cider vinegar
1 t. vanilla extract
4-inch cinnamon stick

6 whole cloves
1 orange, thinly sliced
Garnish: caramel ice cream
    topping

Combine all ingredients except caramel topping in a slow cooker. Cover and cook on low setting for 5 to 6 hours. Discard orange slices and spices. Serve cider in hot mugs, drizzling a teaspoon of caramel topping into each mug. Makes 16 servings.

Serve up apple slices with this yummy dip. Blend together an 8-ounce package of softened cream cheese with 3/4 cup packed brown sugar and one teaspoon vanilla extract.

OVER THE RIVER
& Through the Woods

Favorite Childhood Memories

Jean McKinney
Ontario, OH

I grew up in the small town of Shelby, Ohio. Every fall our elementary class bundled up and walked from the school to the local public library uptown. Dried leaves crunched under our feet as we made the trek. I remember feeling the cool, crisp air, the warmth of the sun on my cheeks and the explosion of color in all the fall leaves. Afterwards we stopped by the local bakery, where we each enjoyed a small carton of orange juice and a giant pumpkin-shaped cookie decorated with orange frosting. I have other sweet fall memories too. Beyond my family's backyard was a parking lot for the grocery store and the bowling alley. Back then it seemed the town closed down on Sunday. For us kids, it was our favorite day because we had this huge parking lot to ride our bicycles in. We would spend hours on our bikes riding up & down the parking lot. Our imaginations ran wild...one week it might have been our town, the next Sunday it was the moon, the beach or California. But the part I will forever cherish is coming into the house cold and tired afterwards, when Mom had hot cocoa waiting for us. Mom is gone now, but I have carried on those sweet memories and traditions with my own children. And every fall I still treat myself to a pumpkin cookie with a glass of orange juice.

OVER THE RIVER
& Through the Woods

~~~~~~

Cider Mill Memories

Diana Lew
Colorado Springs, CO

I grew up in what is now Auburn Hills, Michigan. Every fall my family took a drive on a long dirt road in the country to Yates Cider Mill in Rochester Hills, Michigan. The trees would be ablaze with beautiful colors and the air was crisp and fresh. As we arrived at the mill, a large waterwheel powered by a stream would be turning to run the cider press inside. As we entered, we saw the the giant press mashing the apples. The scent of freshly pressed cider and freshly baked old-fashioned doughnuts greeted us. There's nothing like fresh cider and doughnuts on a beautiful fall day! Here in Colorado I have Pike's Peak and the Rockies to greet me everyday, but when fall comes I still long for a trip back to Michigan and that cider mill.

Harvest Moon Dinnertime

Kelly Turk
Benson, AZ

I recall the full moon at dusk while I was growing up in Conrad, northern Montana, in late August of winter wheat harvest time. Rising over the hills, the moon looked like a huge glowing orange pumpkin. While the hired men, combine and truck drivers washed off grain chaff for dinner at the patio, I would be at the barn unsaddling my horse after checking the cattle, the sweet grassy scent of hay filling my lungs. The excitement grew for the terrific meal laid out by Mom and my older sisters for the crew, delectable aromas drifting in. Dad called us to "come and get it." The only time of year we had pie every night after dinner was during harvest. Tonight it would be fresh peach pie after a dinner of roast beef and fresh garden vegetables, lightly steamed, with herbs and rich, thick melting butter. Our family gathered with the crew and enjoyed the last night outdoors for dinner before autumn swept in. A bit of melancholy set in for me, as in one week I would be starting high school...oh my, such memories!

Fruit-Picking Time

Beckie Apple
Grannis, AR

My grandparents on my dad's side raised 11 children on a large farm in the rural community of Blue Ball, Arkansas. My dad, born in 1934, was the next to youngest. Their life was a true American legend of hard work and wonderful rewards. They had every kind of farm animal and raised all their family's food crops. Grampa had huge fields of cotton, corn and sorghum, a large fruit orchard of apples, pears, peaches and of course enough vegetables in the garden to support his large family. I remember the fruit-picking time and all the excitement that it brought to me and my brother. We got to ride in the horse-pulled wagon as the fruit was picked and loaded. Our job was to keep the baskets pulled to the front of the wagon...and to eat as much fruit as we could get away with! I loved to watch Gramp making the sorghum molasses just as much. I will cherish these memories forever.

OVER THE RIVER
& Through the Woods

Fall Leaves in the Mountains

Connie Shortel
Orlando, FL

Autumn has always been my favorite time of year. My birthday is in October, right around Columbus Day. When I was growing up in Sissonville, West Virginia, we never had Columbus Day off from school, but my father always had it off. And every year he'd let me take my birthday off and we'd go to the mountains to see the leaves. I love the changing leaves, the crispness of fall with a hint of smoke. That's the thing I miss most, now that I live in Florida. So, a couple of years ago, with my kids being old enough to leave alone, I went home and on my birthday got to travel all through the mountains with my father again. What a sweet time it was!

Annual Harvest Party

Kristie Rigo
Friedens, PA

Every year my husband and I host a harvest party for our church. We've been holding these fun gatherings for the past six or seven years, usually on the first Saturday in October when the leaves are vibrant, the air is crisp and the weather is suitable for sweatshirts. While the guests mingle, my husband builds a roaring bonfire, and we cook a huge kettle of vegetable beef soup outside. There's something about soup cooked in a cast-iron kettle over an outdoor fire that makes it extra yummy! Everyone brings their favorite side dish or dessert to go along with the soup. You'll find homemade dinner rolls and apple crisp almost every year. After dinner you may find us splitting up into teams and heading out for a scavenger hunt, or loading up on a wagon for an old-fashioned hayride. No matter what, we always have fun and can't wait to do it again next year.

First Grade in a Three-Room School   *Delores Lakes*
Mansfield, OH

I grew up in Harrisonburg, Virginia, out in the country. My first two years of elementary school, in the late 1950s, were spent at the same three-room school my grandparents had attended back in the early 1900s. There was a tradition that on a sunny day each fall, the first and second-graders would walk to the woods half a mile from the school to have a picnic lunch, then play games afterwards. We never knew which day was to be chosen for this event, but it was greatly anticipated. I remember so well marching single file toward those woods, lunchbox in hand. The crisp fall air, the bright sunny sky and the colorful leaves crunching underfoot all seemed so exciting and special to me, doing fun things with my classmates. The students in the upper grades would always say, "There goes Cox's Army" when they saw our teacher, Miss Cox, leading the little group of children for their fall outing. What a wonderful memory this is to me, 55 years later.

Apple Butter Makin' Time

Terri Bary
DePauw, IN

Each year in the fall, when those delicious apples have ripened to perfection, it's apple butter makin' time here in Indiana. For the past 23 years, my husband's family has made apple butter. We begin early in the morning with just a few helpers to peel, core and quarter the apples. Then mid-morning the fire is lit under a huge copper-plated kettle. Time to get those apples cooking! By now, many other family members and friends begin to drift in, knowing that there will be an abundance of food. Everyone brings a little something for a pitch-in. Soups, hot dogs, barbecue, sweet rolls, pies, cookies, cakes and candies...as you can tell, this family loves sweets! There's homemade bread or biscuits for tasting that delicious apple butter when it reaches its final stages. Everyone visits, eats and yes, takes their turn at stirring the butter with that big ol' wooden paddle. When the apples have cooked to the right consistency, the sugar, cinnamon oil and red hots are added. Everyone gets a little taste to see if it is just right, but the final word comes from the head man. My father-in-law, who has been doing this since he was a child, makes the final decision that it is, indeed, apple butter! At that time the kettle is removed from the fire. Then it goes to the family assembly line, where one person ladles the apple butter into a pint jar, another carefully cleans the top, then the next one lays a piping-hot lid on the jar, and finally the last one gets to put on the jar ring for its final seal. After all is done, the men clean up the big kettle and the women clean up what little is left from the pitch-in. Everyone gets to take a few jars of the delicious apple butter home with them. It is so neat to hear those jars popping, saying that the day's work is done. But the best part is the family tradition we are keeping for our children, and of course the many new memories that are made each year!

Harvesting Grandma's Garden

Sharon Leach
Two Rivers, WI

My grandma always had a big garden at her home in Spencer, Wisconsin, and every fall I would help her. We dug up potatoes, carrots, beets and onions. Carrots were always put in sand, onions always hung up to dry. Beets were pickled and canned. She cut off the cabbages from their stems, shredded them into crocks and made sauerkraut. And oh my, the pickles that were made! I picked little apples for home-canned candied apples. To this day, I can still see us in her garden getting all the veggies dug up and getting them ready for winter. Much later I realized how much hard work it was for her then, but it was fun for me!

Treats for the Sheep

Judith Fintel
Deshler, NE

My husband has begun a little tradition with our grandsons Jacob and Jonathan over the past few years. We live on an acreage and have a few sheep. The farmers raise corn in the fields around us. When the little boys (ages seven and five now) come to visit in the fall, they go on a little walk in the field with Gramps. They look for ears of corn the combine harvester has missed and bring them to the sheep for a special treat. The first year they did this, they didn't think to bring a sack to carry the ears in, so they stuffed them into their little pockets and carried them in their arms. It was sweet to see the little boys loaded down with all those ears in the anticipation of bringing goodies to the sheep. They have done this for about three years now, and it has become a fun tradition they look forward to doing with their grandpa.

OVER THE RIVER
& Through the Woods

Homecoming Parade

Cyndy DeStefano
Mercer, PA

We live in a small town where there is only one red light, but we are big in spirit. Each year for homecoming, our school invites alumni to participate in a parade to showcase all of our fall sports and of course the homecoming court. The parade only goes about three blocks but kicks off the homecoming football game. Past band members are invited to march right along with our current band, which is the largest in the county in spite of our school being one of the smallest. The opposing team's band is invited to participate in the parade as well and often does so. Past majorettes and dance line members are also invited. The streets are lined with people, young and old, returning alumni and newcomers as well. We often stop at a store along the way for a cup of pumpkin spice cappuccino to sip as the parade goes by. Each year our little parade seems to grow. We think it is to keep up with our hometown pride which grows right along with it!

Bonfire Wiener Roasts

Gail Kelsey
Phoenix, AZ

My mom's birthday was in mid-October. She always had wonderful memories of wiener roasts with a large bonfire on her birthday when she was a teenager. After my sister and I were born in Kewanee, Illinois, we moved to Arizona and the big city, where bonfires aren't allowed. Fortunately we had some older cousins who owned a dairy farm on the outskirts of town. We loved going there for many celebrations, but the wiener roast for Mom's birthday was one of the best. The nights began to get cooler from the hot summers, and we knew that the fall season was finally just around the corner. Mom passed away last year and the city has grown past the farmland, but I will have these memories forever.

Church Homecomings

Rita Frye
King, NC

We celebrate homecoming at our church every September, after the humidity of the southern summer has subsided. Our tradition is to shop for the homecoming meal on Friday evening, then cook all day Saturday. Homecomings have grown so much that we can't all fit in the Fellowship Hall. So, the men erect a huge tent in the field out beside the sanctuary. There are always gasps of delight when everyone makes the turn into the church parking lot and sees that huge tent with seemingly endless tables of food set up underneath. Somehow, it appears even more massive against the crisp, blue autumn sky! The fellowship during the worship service and afterward at the meal on the grounds is always so sweet! It's precious to see faces who have moved away and are just back for the day. Some of these visitors are my children, who have married and started families of their own. I love to just sit and watch the children play in the field as the cool fall breezes blow beneath the tent. Has it really been that many years since I was balancing a plate for a toddler with a baby on my hip? Precious memories of the day, precious memories of homecomings of so many years past.

Raking Leaves with Daddy

Jane Anderson
Surprise, AZ

I grew up in Olympia, Washington. Every year around the first of November and before the first snowfall, Daddy would rake the leaves in our yard. Then he would pile them in the wheelbarrow and set me on top of them. He'd take the wheelbarrow with me on top of the leaves down the hill, where they were picked up to be used for mulch by the farmers in town. This memory has stayed with me for over 60 years.

OVER THE RIVER
& Through the Woods

Potato Harvesting Days

Susan St. Amand
Strasburg, VA

I grew up many years ago in Van Buren, Maine, a small rural farming town on the border of Canada. School would let out from mid-September until mid-October for the students and their families to help the farmers harvest their potato crops. Most of us used our harvest earnings to buy new school clothes that we couldn't afford, or save for Christmas shopping, which was right around the corner. Harvest days were long, cool fall days that began soon after sunrise and ended toward sundown. The potatoes were picked by hand into baskets, then dumped into barrels to be picked up by flatbed trucks. We looked forward to lunch breaks in the field, when we enjoyed the packed lunches that Mom prepared for us. This was one of the few times of the year that she did a lot of baking and it all ended up in our lunchpails. The best of the baked goods would be her homemade whoopie pies. At the end of the day, after a long day out in the dirt picking potatoes, a hot bath never felt so good! We would rejoice on the rare occasions when it rained and we could take a day off from the potato picking. During the four weeks of harvest, we witnessed the changing fall colors of the trees and eventually the barren trees. At times, if we were lucky, a stray deer or moose would cross the fields. Then came the honking of Canada geese flying overhead in their V-shaped formation, heading south for the winter. Years have passed, and I have since moved to Virginia. During the winters here, I see many Canada geese landing here on their journey south, and still think of my younger days and potato harvests back in Maine.

Nature Walks With Grandpa

Angela Bissette
Zebulon, NC

Growing up in Wilson, North Carolina, every autumn I enjoyed nature walks with my grandpa. As soon as the weather changed and the leaves started falling, I knew it was time. We would explore the woods for hours. Grandpa would show me all the different plants and trees, tell me the names of them and even which ones were edible or medicinal. He showed me the tracks of small animals and helped me learn to identify them. We would sit quietly, just listening to the birds and watching the squirrels collecting their food for winter. Our favorite part of our walk was finding a wild scuppernong grapevine and having a little snack before heading home. Grandpa taught me to enjoy and respect nature, and I treasure the memory of those fun times we had together.

Harvest Haywagon Rides

Lois Jones
Michigan City, IN

I grew up in the tiny town of Hinsdale, New York, in a house that was in our family for many, many generations. It's very quaint and beautiful there in the fall with the trees changing colors. Some of my favorite memories are of all the rides on the haywagons as we worked the fields of our small farm. I loved the smell of fresh-cut crops that lingered on the wagons. But the best thing of all was waiting for us when we returned to the farm. Grandmother would have an amazing soup ready to warm us up after being outside in the cool fall air all day. She used her own home-grown root vegetables, and the soup smelled so good as we came inside after a long day of working. It was always followed by a fresh, warm slice of apple or pumpkin pie...yum!

204

Bonfires at the Farm

Diane Price
Nappanee, IN

Fall brings back such sweet memories of my childhood in Plymouth, Indiana. The first signs of the season were pumpkins and mums scattered around the lawn under the trees and on the open porch. A pair of Dad's tattered old bib overalls always made the perfect scarecrow, with holes in the knees where the straw would pop through. Our scarecrow would have one arm raised as if it were waving at passersby. I fondly remember one farming family who would often drive by on their tractors...each year when they spotted the scarecrow, they would wave, thinking it was my dad waving at them! Bonfires were the highlight of the crisp autumn nights, especially around Halloween when we had family, friends and neighbors attending. Bales of straw would encircle the dancing flames from the fire, as people sat upon them sipping old-fashioned apple cider. There's just nothing like weenies and s'mores over an open fire. Afterwards, we would go on our hayride across the creek and through the woods. I will always cherish these memories of growing up on the farm.

Harvest Treat Drop-Off

Nicole Culver
La Fontaine, IN

My family's best harvest-time tradition is to make a big batch of different goodies and package them up nicely, then put them into trick-or-treat buckets. One night in October, we wait until it gets nice and dark, then we drive several blocks across town near our friends' houses. My boys jump out of the van and they walk another block. Then the boys set the treat bucket on the porch, knock loudly and run as fast as they can back to the van. We enjoy doing this so much that we've incorporated it into several other holidays throughout the year. It may take the recipients a few times until they figure out it was us...but we continue to do it because it's so much fun!

Halloween Costumes Past

Jane Robinson
Driftwood, TX

My hometown of Scottsbluff, Nebraska is on the high plains and has some of the prettiest sunsets you'll ever see! When I was young, every autumn was an adventure...the beginning of school, weekend football games, cool evenings and the anticipation of upcoming holidays. It was never too early to start planning my Halloween wardrobe. My costume was always something unusual and, since my mother sewed nearly everything I wore, the sky was almost the limit. From Southern Belle to an old-fashioned swimsuit (complete with bloomers!) to a Japanese lady, I was a lucky little girl. My mother has always said that Halloween was hardly over before I was planning the next year's costume. What a wonderful part of childhood that was!

Apple Picking & Doughnuts

Randi Waldvogel
Peach Bottom, PA

Apple picking is a tradition we share as a family and look forward to every autumn. We have so many wonderful memories of traveling to the orchard and helping our son and daughter pick apples of all different varieties and colors. There was also a little market that sold the most scrumptious homemade doughnuts...we had to buy a dozen just for the ride home! As the years have gone by and our children have gotten older, we still set aside a day to go apple picking. Now our children not only pick their own apples, but help us pick ours, too. And yes, we still stop by the little market and buy a dozen of those scrumptious doughnuts for the ride home!

OVER THE RIVER
& Through the Woods

Autumn Excursions

Sonja McNamara
Kewdale, Australia

I am a born and bred West Virginia girl, but following my heart and my beloved husband, I am now in Australia. My most favorite and most missed tradition is what I liked to call my autumn excursions. At the first hint of the changing of the seasons, I loved to get into my car and travel all the back roads of rural West Virginia where I lived. I would take my time and soak in the sights of the changing leaves, the crispness in the air and squirrels scurrying around in search of nuts. I loved the different scents of autumn, letting me know that soon the first crystal flakes of snow would be falling, leading to my most beloved holiday...Christmas! Even though I cannot do that now, as we do not have the same seasons in Australia, I still can remember the sights and smells of autumn.

Autumn Fun in the Country

Wendy Cosgrove
Tallahassee, FL

I remember autumn as a child, living in the small country town of Fletcher, Ohio. Autumn meant church hayrides, hot cider and doughnuts. We would always have a bonfire, too, because the weather was nippy then. My family of eight would go apple picking, and Mom would make homemade applesauce, apple pies, spiced apple rings...the house smelled so delicious! The leaves were turning and falling, and we six kids all took turns raking them up in big piles and then jumping in them! We picked the pumpkins from Dad's garden, and after Mom scooped out the insides to make pumpkin pies and pumpkin butter, we got to carve them. Autumn was a fun time for me as a child, I sure do miss those simple days!

Pumpkin Carving Time

Lisa Reed
Chubbuck, ID

Fall is my family's favorite season for many reasons. We share lots of activities during this time as a family, like hunting, fishing, country drives to see the changing leaves and pumpkin carving. When the kids were little, we would pile in the car and drive up the canyon to Frazier's Chicken Farm, where they sold apples from their orchard and pumpkins galore. My husband is like a little kid when it comes to pumpkins, choosing numerous pumpkins for all his ideas! Each year, one of our goals was to find a pumpkin bigger than the year before. I remember him trying to lug this 130-pound pumpkin into the van. We managed to get it in and all four kids too! What a fun evening, with old sheets spread all over the floor as all six of us began to clean out our pumpkins. There would be pumpkin guts everywhere! And then choosing a pattern...what fun to watch as everyone poked their pattern onto their pumpkin. Then we would line them up on the porch for the lighting of the pumpkins. Sometimes we had up to 15 pumpkins glowing on our little porch. People would drive by and stop just to see them. As the kids have gotten older and busier, our tradition has dwindled. I hope it is something that will be rekindled when the grandkids come along. It wasn't so much about the pumpkins, but the hours that were spent together laughing and enjoying each other's company.

Halloween Happiness

Dina Willard
Abingdon, MD

When our girls were younger, they always looked forward to hosting a big neighborhood Halloween party at our home. An hour before trick-or-treat, all the ghosts and goblins would gather around a spooky-themed feast. Dressed in my best witch's hat, I'd serve up bubbling brew, mummy wraps, skeleton fingers, crunchy bat wings and dip, toad tongue and of course platters of sweet treats. It was enough to feed a whole army of monster bellies! At exactly 6 o'clock the real magic would begin. My husband would tag along as the whole neighborhood filled with princesses and pirates who were running up & down the leaf-filled streets. Many homes including our next-door neighbors went all out with the creepy decorations. After a couple hours of tricks or treats, all the little spooks would come back with pillowcases bursting at the seams with every imaginable confection. They'd dump it all on the floor and have a great time swapping their loot with their friends. At 9 o'clock the party was over. The mess was cleared away and all the candles blown out, except one…our Jack-o'-Lantern, which stayed lit well into the evening to scare away any real ghosts!

Welcome, October!

Cindy Wilson-Rocco
Danbury, CT

The first Friday night of every October, my daughters and I have a tradition of watching scary movies together and bringing out all of our Halloween decorations. When my girls were younger, I would make hot dog mummies and popcorn for us to snack on. Now that they are teenagers, they each pick an appetizer to make. Once we are finished decorating, we enjoy the appetizers they prepared and share hot cocoa together. No matter how busy we are, we all look forward to our night together and our official start of the Halloween season!

Trick-or-Treat Map

Heidi Caldwell
New Plymouth, ID

I grew up in the small, rural town of Hines, Oregon. Every year for Halloween my brother and I would sit down and map out our trick-or-treat plan before the big day, trying to figure out the best route to take in order to maximize filling our pumpkins. Of course we knew which house served the popcorn balls, which one had scary decorations and which one had spooky music playing. We always made sure those houses were first on the plan! When the big day came, we would rush home from school, put on our costumes (always homemade by Mom) and head out to gather as much candy as we could. I am now 34, and every year the memories of my childhood trick-or-treat map give me warm feelings on Halloween.

OVER THE RIVER
& Through the Woods

Small-Town Halloween

Lynda Lingg
Huber Heights, OH

My small-town Halloween was a great experience and a wonderful memory for me. I grew up in College Corner, a little town that sits on the Indiana-Ohio state line. When I was young, the whole town made quite a big deal out of Halloween, with a festival and many more activities. I remember seeing some of my guy friends trying to catch greased pigs or climb the greased pole in the center of the town's ball field. It was hilarious! The town also had costume contests as well as best-dressed pet contests. My family and I went to the town's firehouse for a fish fry with our whole community. It was such a warm and loving atmosphere in which everyone knew everybody else. The kids always knew which house gave out what homemade treat on trick-or-treat night. I remember running across town for the best popcorn balls ever. Now I live in the suburbs of a city, and it's just not the same. I really miss those small-town days!

Pumpkin Rescue

Kristina Clayton
Seven Fields, PA

My favorite fall memory is going to the Pumpkin Patch every year with my father. But instead of searching for the most round, perfect pumpkin, we do the opposite! We try to pick out a pumpkin that's lopsided, oddly colored or has an unusual stem, then do our best job to make it pretty. By either painting, carving or other craft mediums, we try to use our imagination and make something really unique. It's sort of a "pumpkin rescue mission," and it's lots of fun!

211

Pumpkin Patch Memories

Melissa Dattoli
Richmond, VA

I love going to the pumpkin patch in Ashland, Virginia as much today as I did when I was a child. The hayrides and warm cider bring back wonderful memories of hours spent trying to find the perfect pumpkin. Our local pumpkin patch always had a special challenge...if you could carry six pumpkins for six feet, you got one pumpkin free! Year after year, my brothers and I piled pumpkins on our poor dad and laughed as we watched him and all the other dads trying to carry all those pumpkins six feet. A few years, Dad managed to get the free pumpkin, but the memories of those days are far more valuable! I still go there to get our pumpkins for carving.

A Spooky, Smoky Dinner

Kristi Adducci
Arvada, CO

Several years ago we got a smoke machine at the Halloween store. A week before our actual party, we started our "practice" Halloween dinner. Everything was beautiful...the spooky decorated table, the hanging skeleton, the pumpkins, everything. Then we turned on the smoke machine. I think we may have gone a little crazy, because you could no longer see the table, the decorations or the food. Guess we should have read the instructions! However, we adjusted the smoke machine and the actual party was perfect for our guests, with just enough smoke to make the atmosphere.

Thanksgiving Snow

Mary Moore
Nova Scotia, Canada

It was the mid-late 1970s when an unexpected October snowstorm hit Nova Scotia on the Thanksgiving weekend and dumped several feet of snow, knocking out power for several days. My two older sisters had come home for the holiday, and one of them brought along her new boyfriend. What a great first impression that was for him! Mum had purchased the turkey and all the items necessary for the perfect Thanksgiving dinner. No power? No cooking? No dinner? Not so! My enterprising mum sent Dad out into the storm to find fuel for the camp stove and the lamps. I honestly don't know how she managed it, but she cooked an entire Thanksgiving dinner for seven people on a two-burner camp stove!

For this,
We are blessed
The love of company,
The company of friends
and all the abundance
of Autumn.

Old Blessing

Secret Shopper

Beth Cassinos
Silver Springs, NV

I have a special ritual every Thanksgiving Eve that I look forward to. I share this tradition with my friend Kristen, who lives across the country in Massachusetts. I love to go grocery shopping for my last-minute menu items in the midst of all the hustle & bustle of the crowds. I only pick up about ten items so it's not too hectic. I love to see what's in everybody's carts and try to guess what they are making. Sure, there are cranky people out there, but I mostly focus on the families, all a-chatter about the holiday. Sometimes I even overhear a secret family recipe or two! Once I get home, I send a message to my friend. We share our experiences and sometimes even a picture or two of what we put in our carts. It may sound a little silly, but it's a tradition I can't do without!

Home for Thanksgiving

Sonya Crain
Jonesborough, TN

Growing up as the daughter of a Master Sergeant in the United States Air Force, to say we moved a lot is an understatement. But come November, it didn't matter where we were living at the time, I knew where I would be on Thanksgiving. My family always came home for Thanksgiving. That home was my mother's parents' home in Oldtown, Maryland...Pap-Pap's & Grandma's, the place where my aunts & uncles and all my cousins would be. Even now that I am grown and living away from my family, my cousins have families of their own and we live all over the United States, we still all come home for that wonderful holiday, Thanksgiving. We celebrate that joyous time of year together with turkey and all the trimmings. We are truly blessed, and I wouldn't miss it for anything.

Dad's Work Turkey

Kimberly Fought
Livonia, MI

My father's employer used to give each family a turkey the day before Thanksgiving. I would run to the door of our home in Detroit to watch my father carry in the turkey and see how big this year's bird was. My mother would get up in the wee hours on Thanksgiving morning to cook that prized turkey. Then our family piled into the car and carted this delicious dish to my aunt's house for a family gathering so large my aunt had already roasted a second turkey. My mom and aunt sliced the turkeys and piled the slices high on a platter. Every side dish imaginable and, of course, the two turkeys were enjoyed by my numerous cousins, aunts & uncles. I remember sitting at the kids' table and just feeling overwhelmed with family and incredible food...and proud that everyone was enjoying the same bird Dad had carried in the front door the day before.

Kids' Holiday Tradition

Susan French
Knob Noster, MO

When our children were small, we began a new tradition for our holiday meals. We allowed each child to pick out two of their favorite foods to have at the holiday meal, then they helped make the dishes they had chosen. This ensured that there would be at least two dishes at the holiday table that each child loved, and they would know how to prepare their favorite foods. The tradition grew as our family grew, and with seven kids (some grown and some still young), our tradition is that if you are going to be home for the holiday dinner, then you still get to pick out your two dishes. Usually the kids away from home will call to see who picked what dish to go with our holiday meal. It's a wonderful tradition for all of us.

No Gravy!

Lori Williams
Acton, ME

As my siblings and I grew up and got married, we began taking
holidays as our own, hosting the whole family at our houses rather
than having Mom do all the work. My sister Rae claimed Thanksgiving
as her holiday, and so that year we gathered at her house in Sanford,
Maine. Of course the delicious aroma of turkey roasting all day and the
pies set out to remind us to save room for dessert were just as enjoyable
as the family visiting and sharing good times. When it was nearly time
to serve dinner, our Grammy took to making the gravy. She used the
pan drippings from the turkey, of course, and asked my sister for flour.
Stirring and stirring, she wondered why it wasn't thickening up...then
she tasted it and discovered what was wrong. Through her laughter she
tried to tell us that she wasn't given flour but powdered sugar! Sadly
there was no gravy that year, but we did have lots of laughs and happy
memories of one of our last Thanksgivings with Gram. I have since
claimed Thanksgiving as my holiday, and though our Grammy isn't
with us anymore, I use her silver at Thanksgiving, and we always
remember the year we had no gravy!

OVER THE RIVER
& Through the Woods

Thanksgiving Weekend Fun

Janis Rooney
Parker, CO

Every year our family's Thanksgiving weekend is jam-packed with activities. It starts with Thanksgiving Day, when we have as many as 20 family members together. On Friday, we all go to a holiday movie together, then everyone comes back to our house for leftovers. So we have to make enough food to provide two days' dinners for 20 people! Saturday is our favorite day, when we all go up to the same mountain every year and cut down our Christmas trees. With five families looking for trees, we all help each other find that perfect one. Some of us even get two trees to place in different rooms in our homes. We bring a picnic lunch and spend the whole day together. After everyone has found their trees, we go home and again share a meal together, usually soups and chili. On Sunday, we all stay at our homes and decorate our own special Christmas tree. Every year we hardly change a thing...it's our favorite weekend of the whole year.

Dad's Thanksgiving Grace

Nancy Christensen
Prairie City, IA

My dad, who was a WWII vet, loved to write poems for all occasions...
this is one of them.

Giving Thanks

Blessed be this family,
Gathered here today.
Each of us feels the love that's here,
But feels no need to say.
Now as we bless this food
In its many dishes,
We know the gravy is delicious
And the cranberries are so bold
So let's get to eatin'
'Cause the turkey is gettin' cold!

INDEX

INDEX

INDEX

Have a taste for more?

We created our official Circle of Friends so we could
fill everyone in on the latest scoop at once.
Visit us online to join in the fun and discover free
recipes, exclusive giveaways and much more!

www.gooseberrypatch.com

Call us toll-free at 1·800·854·6673

U.S. to Metric Recipe Equivalents

Volume Measurements

1/4 teaspoon	1 mL
1/2 teaspoon	2 mL
1 teaspoon	5 mL
1 tablespoon = 3 teaspoons	15 mL
2 tablespoons = 1 fluid ounce	30 mL
1/4 cup	60 mL
1/3 cup	75 mL
1/2 cup = 4 fluid ounces	125 mL
1 cup = 8 fluid ounces	250 mL
2 cups = 1 pint =16 fluid ounces	500 mL
4 cups = 1 quart	1 L

Weights

1 ounce	30 g
4 ounces	120 g
8 ounces	225 g
16 ounces = 1 pound	450 g

Oven Temperatures

300° F	150° C
325° F	160° C
350° F	180° C
375° F	190° C
400° F	200° C
450° F	230° C

Baking Pan Sizes

Square

8x8x2 inches	2 L = 20x20x5 cm
9x9x2 inches	2.5 L = 23x23x5 cm

Rectangular

13x9x2 inches	3.5 L = 33x23x5 cm

Loaf

9x5x3 inches	2 L = 23x13x7 cm

Round

8x1-1/2 inches	1.2 L = 20x4 cm
9x1-1/2 inches	1.5 L = 23x4 cm